WATERLOO HIGH SCHOOL LIBRARY
1464 INDUSTRY RD.
ATWATER, OHIO 44201

The Great Bull Market

THE NORTON ESSAYS IN AMERICAN HISTORY

Under the general editorship of

HAROLD M. HYMAN

William P. Hobby Professor of American History
Rice University

WATERLOO HIGH SCHOOL LIBRARY
1464 INDUSTRY RD.
ATWATER, OHIO 44201

The Great
Bull Market

Wall Street in the 1920s

Robert Sobel

W · W · NORTON & COMPANY

New York · London

332.6
Sob

W. W. Norton & Company, Inc., 500 Fifth Avenue, New York, N.Y. 10110
W. W. Norton & Company Ltd., 25 New Street Square, London EC4A 3NT

Library of Congress Catalog Card No. 68-19795
Copyright © 1968 by W. W. Norton & Company, Inc. All rights reserved.

Printed in the United States of America.
ISBN 0-393-09817-6
8 9 0

For David

Contents

Introduction

〰〰〰〰〰〰〰〰〰〰〰〰〰〰〰〰〰〰〰〰〰〰〰〰〰〰

IN HIS preface to *The Waning of the Middle Ages,* Johan Huizinga stated: "History has always been far more engrossed by problems of origins than by those of decline and fall. When studying any period, we are always looking for the promise of what the next is to bring." This is true of the decade of the twenties in American history. To many historians it offers what William Leuchtenberg has called "the perils of prosperity," and the prelude to the New Deal. Presidents Harding, Coolidge, and Hoover become interludes between Wilson and Roosevelt, men who attempted to return to the McKinley era. "Normalcy" and the kind of society it stood for often becomes a frothy period between the New Freedom and the New Deal. It is presented as a freakish age, filled with people like Babe Ruth, Texas Guinan, Legs Diamond, Jimmy Walker, H. L. Mencken, Charles Lindbergh and Peaches Browning. Politicians are viewed as paunchy men in cream-colored suits or demagogues with Indian feathers. The Sacco-Vanzetti trial is treated soberly, but the Scopes trial becomes a circus in the hands of many writers. And above all there is Prohibition, the experiment that failed, which in failing cast a spell of false hilarity over the age. For most Americans, the twenties are not to be taken seriously.

But this is not true of one event of the decade: the 1929 stock market crash. Like the Battle of Marathon, the assassination of Julius Caesar, the voyage of Columbus, and the storming of the Bastille, it has entered the realm of mythology and semi-truth, no longer studied as an historical event, but more as a

symbol of greater forces and new beginnings. Just as contemporaries of George Washington and Abraham Lincoln
would not recognize them in our images of them today, so
those directly involved in the events of October 1929 seem
caricatures rather than flesh-and-blood humans. If we are
properly to learn the importance of such events and individuals,
myths must be stripped away, and the actual happenings studied
and understood in their contexts. In order to appreciate the
meaning of the events of 1929, one must review the entire
bull market from 1921 onward, see its relationships with other
aspects of American life in the period, and attempt to understand the dynamics and mechanisms of the securities markets.
Huizinga was correct. Historians are concerned with "problems
of origins," but they must remember that all origins are also
conclusions of previous periods.

Such a perspective is doubly important for the study of the
1929 panic. In the summer of 1967 John Kenneth Galbraith,
author of *The Great Crash,* deplored the fact that his was the
only book dealing with the subject, while there were three on
the atomic device lost off the Spanish coast. This indicates,
said Galbraith, that American historians have not paid sufficient
attention to what is truly important in the nation's experience.
Galbraith is incorrect. Although his is the most famous book
on the subject, there are a scattering of others, as well as much
material written in the period. The crash was like some huge
whale washed up on the beach to writers of the thirties. They
looked at it from all sides, and wrote of their findings. Similarly,
the bull market of the twenties was exciting and important to
Americans of that decade, and they too published works on
the subject. There is a rich and revealing bibliography on the
crash, which will be discussed at the end of this volume.

Galbraith wrote that "as a year, 1929 has always been
peculiarly the property of economists." [1] Unfortunately, this is
true. Economists have dug deeply into the event, and have

1. John K. Galbraith. *The Great Crash: 1929* (Boston, 1961), p. 2.

done much to enlighten us as to its meaning. But, as Huizinga indicated, economists and historians do not ask the same questions. Historians want to know more about causes and effects. What led up to the bull market? How did it develop? Why did it attract as many people as it did? What were the weaknesses in the system, and how did they begin and grow? What men were responsible for significant events of the period, how did they get into these positions of power, and why did they act the way they did? How did contemporaries view the crash? What were its results, bad and good? These are questions historians inevitably ask, and they have not been answered in most books on the subject.

This leads to another, more serious problem. Since the crash was so important, it is only natural to view the market actions of the twenties in such a way as to trace its origins. In Galbraith's and other works we see the inexorable march toward disaster, but not the imponderables that appeared to participants. One gets the impression that speculators in the summer of 1929 were either stupid or blind not to have realized what was coming. In fact, they were neither. Generally speaking, inevitability appears only in retrospect.

In this regard, students of the stock market panic would do well to begin their research by a careful reading of Roy Nichols' masterpiece, *The Disruption of American Democracy,* in which the author writes of the political and economic filigree of the pre–Civil War period. After the first few chapters the reader begins to understand the problems facing America in the 1850s, and the many possibilities for their solution or amelioration. By midbook, it is clear that nothing was pre-ordained in 1859; war was only one course of many. The reader knows what happened, but so great is Nichols' skill that at times one finds himself wondering how the book will end. When and if the student can arrive at this perspective of events, he can say that he understands the problems of the period.

This book was written with these ideas in mind. I have tried to indicate that the crash did not seem inevitable to

Americans of 1929; that stock prices seemed reasonable; that most of today's investors, faced with the kind of market which existed in September 1929 would more likely have been bulls than bears. For that matter, in terms of prices the great bull market of the twenties may seem more justifiable than the striking stock market advances of the post–World War II period. To understand this, one must study not only 1929, but the entire decade.

This book has several theses, which the reader is entitled to know before he starts the first chapter. I believe that stock prices were depressed in 1921–1922, due to the effects of an economic slump, a narrow view of the economy, and an anti-quated philosophy of investment. Thus, the bull market was not only natural, but overdue. Prices did not rise unreasonably in the twenties, though the advance was indeed dramatic. Rather, they reflected a new, more realistic view of the nation's position and prospects after World War I, and the growth in earnings of common stocks.

Secondly, it is my belief that the institutional structure of finance capitalism and the nation's political leadership were inadequate, unable to grasp or come to grips with the nation's problems and possibilities after the war. This led to abuses, mistakes, and excesses. It was, to borrow Ray Ginger's name for a previous period, an "Age of Excess." This has led me to the conclusion that the crash was not caused primarily by a runaway market but, more importantly, by weaknesses on Wall Street and in Washington, and the creation of an unhealthy nexus between business and speculation, especially in brokers' loans.

I do not think the market collapse of October was as disastrous as we have been led to believe. Contemporary accounts of the crash indicate that participants tended to relate the panic to the sharp declines of 1893 and 1907, and did not consider it a major turning point in American history. In those years the drops in securities prices were sharper than they were in October and the early part of November 1929, before they recovered somewhat. The market rallied for the next six months, and in this period much of the damage caused by the crash, as well as the weaknesses which led to it, might have been corrected. They were not and, as a result, the nation entered a depression which could have been shortened and dampened, if not avoided. Needless to say, the tales of people jumping out of windows and fears of an end to the republic were highly exaggerated.

Most of the abuses of the twenties were rectified by the New Dealers, and the institutional structure of America today bears little resemblance to what existed then. The gross national product of 1929 was $104.4 billion, and *per capita* income was $857. Sometime in the next decade our GNP will top the trillion dollar mark, and *per capita* income today is four times that of 1929. To compare the economy and problems of the late 1960s with those of the late 1920s is to compare the Model "A" Ford to the Mustang. We shall never again see the like of Calvin Coolidge, Andrew Mellon, and Charles Mitchell. Although historians may be guilty of repeating themselves, history never does. We may suffer through panics in the future, but there will never be "another 1929."

THIS WORK benefited from assistance given me by many friends and critics. The late Burton Crane of *The New York Times* in particular stimulated my interest in the mythology of the market crash. Professor Harold Hyman of Rice University, General Editor of this series, read the work with incisive skill, and his criticisms enabled me to overcome some of the pitfalls facing an historian attempting to explain the vagaries of Wall Street to other historians. Professor Broadus Mitchell of New College, Hofstra University, read parts of the manuscript, and clarified several thorny points regarding public opinion during the 1920s.

The Great Bull Market

Prelude

IN LATE September of 1919 Charles Ponzi, a forty-two-year-old ex-vegetable dealer, forger, and smuggler, decided he would become a wealthy financier. The handsome, quick-witted Ponzi had only $150 in cash and lacked connections of any kind. But he did have an idea and a knowledge of human cupidity. Ponzi would borrow money without collateral, promising to pay $15 for every $10 left with him for ninety days. He told would-be lenders that he planned to use the money to buy International Postal Union reply coupons overseas, and then send them elsewhere to be redeemed. In this way, he could take advantage of differences in currency quotations to make profits. Ponzi would purchase lire, francs, and drachmas at low market prices and sell them at the higher official ones. What could be safer or simpler? Or more legal? As Ponzi said, no one would suffer from such dealings, and everyone so engaged would emerge rich. He left his job as clerk at the foreign trade house of J. P. Poole and set out on his quest.

At first a trickle of funds reached his Boston office, and then more was given to his firm, the Old Colony Foreign Exchange Company. Ponzi took in all the money offered him and paid principal and interest without fuss or bother. Newspapers picked up the Ponzi story; he became famous overnight. By June 1920 money was coming in at the rate of more than $1 million a week. Branch offices were planned, and Ponzi talked of establishing a string of banks and brokerage houses, and then entering manufacturing. In order to gain additional funds and respectability, he purchased controlling interest in the Hanover Trust Company, and made himself its president. Ponzi bought a large house, equipped with servants and a flashy Locomobile. All of his ambitions seemed realized. He even gained control of J. P. Poole and fired his former employer.

Wherever Ponzi went crowds followed. "You're the greatest Italian of them all!" shouted one group. Ponzi protested weakly, "No, no. Columbus and Marconi. Columbus discovered America. Marconi discovered the wireless." "Yes," came the response, "but you discovered money!"

The Boston district attorney's office began a quiet investigation of Ponzi's Old Colony Foreign Exchange Company, and his other organization, the Securities Exchange Company. City Editor Edward Dunn of the Boston *Post* recognized a sensational story, and began his own inquiry. Among other things, Dunn discovered that less than $75,000 worth of reply coupons were printed in most years, and in 1919 there were only $58,560 worth issued. Everyone knew that Ponzi had taken in millions of dollars, and he claimed to have invested them in the coupons. Clearly, the money had been used for other purposes. Upon later investigation, Dunn learned that Ponzi—using the name Charles Bianchi—had been involved in a remittance racket in Montreal in 1907. Confronted with this evidence, Ponzi denied all and, to prevent a panic, he countered by promising to pay 50 per cent interest on money left with him for forty-five days, rather than the ninety days previously required.

Despite this, Ponzi's operations were closed down on July 26, pending the results of an investigation by the district attorney. Ponzi proclaimed his innocence to all who would listen. Lenders besieged his offices but, true to his word, Ponzi paid them off without a single default. BEWARE OF SPECULATORS, read a sign in the window of the Securities Exchange Company. "Syndicates of money sharks are buying up notes of the Securities Exchange Company at small premiums for the purpose of holding them and collecting 50 per cent interest. They know all my notes will be paid. I warn the public against disposing of my notes at a loss. I shall pay everything in full." Ponzi asserted he was worth more than $12 million, and that he paid out $300,000 in one day without straining his resources. This was true; confidence returned. By early August, Ponzi was again talking of expansion programs, as money continued to come into his offices. The Boston *Post* of August 2 claimed he was insolvent, but even this did not prevent people from pressing their funds on the eager Ponzi.

The end came on August 11. All of Ponzi's companies and offices were closed, never to reopen. In the days that followed it was learned that the dapper financier had purchased a few reply coupons, but used most of the money he received to pay those who presented ninety-day notes. In effect, he was taking in money with one hand and paying out more with the other. Such a scheme could not last for long, unless increasing amounts continued to arrive. Ponzi was bound to collapse when the money ran out.

On August 16, Boston and the nation learned that the Old Colony Foreign Exchange Company had no assets and liabilities of $2,121,895. The search for Ponzi's money continued throughout August, September, and into October; little was ever found. Ponzi was declared insolvent on October 15. "While Mr. Ponzi is not to be classed in the same category with robbers and burglars," said Judge James Olmstead, "he was undoubtedly a clever manipulator who took advantage of the credulity of the investing public, which in this instance is the usurer. The investors who loaned their money for a return of the principal and fifty per cent interest would seem themselves guilty of usury if such existed." Olmstead noted that Ponzi had taken in some $15 million in eight months, and that his books showed a deficit of $5 million; less than $200,000 was eventually recovered from his holdings. Ponzi pleaded guilty to charges of larceny and using the mail to defraud and was sentenced to jail. Thus, the strange "Ponzi scheme" came to an end.[1]

Like all periods of American history, the early post–World War I years had their share of scoundrels and confidence men, as well as those who attempted to use loopholes in the law for their own advantage. Even more famous than Ponzi were those athletes on the "Black Sox," who conspired to throw the 1919 World Series to the Cincinnati Reds. A young boy was said to have asked Shoeless Joe Jackson, White Sox star, whether it was true that he had thrown games. "Say it ain't so, Joe," was the way it came out in the press. But Joe Jackson, like Charles Ponzi, was guilty of his crime.

In May 1920 Wall Street learned of a corner in Stutz Motors. Hundreds were wiped out, and a few fortunes were made. But unlike the Ponzi and Black Sox stories, the Stutz corner did not make the front pages. Allen A. Ryan, the man who engineered the Stutz operation, was an unknown Wall Street figure, of interest to some investors and speculators and a handful of professionals, but to no one else. No American who could claim literacy could escape hearing or reading of Joe Jackson and Charles Ponzi, men still remembered today. But who remembers Allen A. Ryan? This is as it should be, for the Ryan corner lacked the drama of the other actions, and involved the emotions and money of fewer people.

Within several years, however, this would be changed. Wall Street happenings would be followed assiduously by millions who in 1920 cared little about the stock markets. Many who had never before purchased securities would "take a flyer" on one stock or another. The Ponzi scheme affected less than

1. While out on bail pending appeal, Ponzi sold underwater lots in Florida to the unsuspecting, thereby making another small fortune. His appeal was denied, and Ponzi went to jail until 1934, at which time he was deported to Italy. Ponzi immediately joined the fascists and gained positions in the government. He was made business manager for LATI Airlines and sent to Rio de Janeiro, where he became a fixture in the social set. Ponzi died of natural causes in January 1949 and was mourned by the Rio business and social community.

50,000 unsophisticated people. Millions were involved—some directly but most indirectly—in the stock market by the end of the decade. Among their number were highly shrewd, knowledgeable speculators who brought years of experience to the market, and many more who, given the chance, would have eagerly pressed their few dollars upon Charles Ponzi. At first it seemed as though the market rise was a once-in-a-lifetime chance to make money with little or no risk. But as stock market prices continued to rise, many began to believe that the rise would be permanent, that the growth curve would be unending. In prospect, this conclusion was reasonable, for the nation was engaged in a great expansion, profits were rising, and conditions seemed sound. In retrospect, we can see the flaws in the argument, the contradictions in the economy which eventually were reflected on Wall Street. The cult of the stock market was, in the end, the greatest fantasy in an age filled with illusion.

1

The Wall Street
Point of View: 1920

FEW LEADING statesmen and political analysts had expected a major world war in 1914 but, by the end of the first week in August, all Europe was in the midst of the fighting. Most economists thought the war would wreck the American export market, cause Europeans to draw their gold from New York, and generally harm the United States. But exports rose sharply in 1915, and European gold was sent to America to pay for war material and food, as well as for safekeeping. President Wilson believed the war would be limited, and would not involve the United States. Instead, World War I was bloodier than the Napoleonic conflict of a century earlier, and in 1917 Wilson himself was obliged to request a declaration of war against the Central Powers. The Germans asked for an armistice in 1918, and in 1919 Wilson went to Europe in order to help frame a peace treaty which would properly conclude "the war to end war." The United States rejected the treaty and did not join the League of Nations; the peace lasted less than one generation.

Many businessmen and economists predicted a depression for 1918–1919. Europe would repatriate its gold, war industries would close down, servicemen would become a glut on the labor market, and America would return to the recessionary climate of 1913. While it was true that war industries suffered, pent-up consumer buying more than took up the slack, and Europe's need for American capital goods was almost as great as its earlier demand for munitions. The gross national product

WATERLOO HIGH SCHOOL LIBRARY
1464 INDUSTRY RD.
ATWATER, OHIO 44201

of 1919 was $41.8 billion; in the peak year of 1918, it had reached $41.6 billion. The nation's export balance in 1918 was $6.2 billion; in 1919, it was a record $7.9 billion. Soldiers did not find breadlines on their return, but instead discovered that the economy was suffering from a labor shortage.

By midsummer of 1919, then, a careful businessman might have reflected that all the major predictions of those who had authority and were in power had been proven wrong by the events of the previous five years. As an individual, he could note the elusiveness of prophecy, but as a businessman he would have to make his plans based on some assessment of the situation.

Any long-range predictions made in 1919 would have to take the effects of the war into consideration. Germany was crushed, and could not be expected to revive for at least another decade. Britain and France, the winners, were exhausted. Both had lost many foreign markets during the war, France had the task of rebuilding the region between Paris and the German border, and Britain's finances were in poor condition. In contrast, the United States had no reconstruction problems, had captured many foreign markets during the war, and had profited economically from the conflict. In 1914, the United States was the world's leading debtor nation, owing others more than $3.8 billion. Through loans and sales, the nation had become the creditor of Europe to the extent of $12.5 billion by 1919. Industry had been rationalized in America, the antitrust campaign of the Progressive era had been buried, and large-scale enterprise was stronger than ever. The census of 1920 would show that for the first time the nation's rural population was less than 50 per cent of the total. America's cities were growing rapidly, while at the same time mechanization of the farms enabled the countryside to produce more foodstuffs and cotton than before. Having attained the upper hand over the domestic reformers, and now the leading commercial factor in the world, the American businessman was the only major victor of the world war. He could well afford to be sanguine in 1919.

This optimism was reflected on Wall Street. Stock prices fell almost 10 per cent in 1917–1918, as did values on every other major securities market in the world. Then came a strong rally, which led security prices into new high ground. The financial analysts offered hopes of further rises in mid-1919, but by the end of the year openly worried about a more rapid European recovery than expected, inflation, and the possibility of a buyers' strike, followed by a turn in the business cycle. By late December 1919 the averages began to decline, and analysts noted that the American exchanges had not shown the strength of their European counterparts. At this point a securities crash of major proportions began. Before the market turned upward in 1920, it had fallen 41.4 per cent from its high, a point which was not recovered for sixty months.

Common Stock Price Movements in Selected Nations, 1918–1920

NATION	POST-ARMISTICE DECLINE (PER CENT)	MARKET RISE, 1919–1920 (PER CENT)	DECLINE FROM 1920 HIGH TO DECEMBER 1920 (PER CENT)
Canada	4.5	28.5	8.4
France	9.7	80.7	16.1
Italy	27.6	111.8	9.8
United Kingdom	6.7	44.1	9.8
United States	9.4	21.1	24.9

SOURCE: *New York Times,* January 1, 1921.

The stock market decline anticipated the depression of 1920–1921. Gross national product dropped from 1920's $40.1 billion to $37.6 billion a year later. The depression threw more than 4 million out of work, and caused some 100,000 bankruptcies. Almost half a million independent farmers lost their homesteads, and there was talk of revolution in the countryside and on the unemployment lines.

In such a situation it was natural to look for a scapegoat, and one was found with little difficulty. When prices soared in 1919, Federal Reserve officials warned against the dangers of a monetary crisis. During the war the System had worked with the Treasury to aid the mobilization effort, and reluctantly accepted a policy of easy money marked by a low rediscount rate.[1] Now the war was over, and easy money threatened the nation with more inflation, the major enemy of most bankers. In an attempt to curb inflation, the Federal Reserve bankers raised the rediscount rate from 4 to 4¾ per cent in November 1919. Easy money advocates protested that such a move would lead to a depression, as businesses would refuse to expand with borrowing costs so high. But in February 1920 the rate went to 5 per cent, and in March to 5¼; more increases followed, along with sharper criticisms from easy money senators and businessmen. By May the depression had begun, caused more by inventory problems, overexpansion, and runaway prices than by Federal Reserve action. The attacks grew, and several legislators suggested the formation of a joint Congressional committee to investigate the System and suggest changes. Bowing to these and other pressures, the Federal Reserve began to lower the rediscount rate, which was cut from 7 per cent to 4½ per cent in the period from May 9 to November 3, 1920. By then the decline had almost run its course and, just as the high rates were blamed for the depression, so the low rates were credited with the recovery. In this way a major myth of the twenties was born: given an atmosphere of easy

1. The *rediscount rate* is the interest rate the Federal Reserve Bank charges member banks for loans. During the 1920s member banks would use commercial paper as collateral for such loans, a practice known as *rediscounting*. (This practice is no longer followed, and most economists use the term *discount rate* in its place. Since the older expression was more common in the period covered by this work, it will be used throughout.) When the Reserve Bank wishes to curb business activity—such as in periods of inflation—it can raise the rediscount rate. Member banks may follow suit, and so offer higher interest rates to holders of savings accounts and charge higher rates to would-be borrowers. Hopefully, the effect would be to encourage saving and discourage spending. Conversely, the Federal Reserve Bank may lower the rediscount rate in periods of recession, thus discouraging saving while offering loans at low rates to businessmen. This method of dealing with economic difficulties is part of the *monetary* approach to financial policy as opposed to the *fiscal* approach which involves the manipulation of government spending.

money, permanent prosperity and growth were inevitable. Not until 1928 would the Federal Reserve bankers attempt to use monetary policy to control the economy, and by then it would be too late.

Money rates were of vital importance to the stock markets of the early postwar period, even more so than today. Traditionally, a purchaser of stocks or bonds would pay only a fraction of its price in cash, borrowing the rest of the money from a bank, and using the security itself as collateral. Such practices were not confined to speculators; conservative investors would think little of borrowing 50 per cent of the purchase price of a sound security. Ordinarily, an investor would try to obtain a time loan, which would run from three months to a year at a fixed rate of interest and be renewable at the option of both parties. Banks and other financial institutions granting time loans would insist on a minimum of 20 per cent collateral for their loans, and charge a relatively low rate of interest. In 1920, a time loan based on secure holdings could be had for 5 per cent. If money rates rose during the period of the loan, the bank would have to forego whatever additional earnings might have been obtained in other investments. Should rates fall, however, the lender might find himself paying 5 per cent when funds were available at 4 per cent or less. In either case, the time loan enabled both parties to count on a definite return for the life of the contract. Almost half the securities loans of 1913 were of this type.

During and after the war, time loans lost ground to call, or demand, loans. A call loan was obtained for a period of one day, and was renewable at the option of both parties at varying rates each business day. Speculators preferred call loans since they were more interested in in-and-out transactions than investments. Such individuals could take advantage of low rates to purchase stocks which otherwise might have been beyond their grasp. Their activities could be magnified many times; call money was often available at less than 20 per cent collateral since the banks could call in their funds in a matter of hours should the market fall. Financial institutions also preferred call loans. By entering the call money market, they could find individuals willing to pay interest on extremely short-term advances, thus enabling the banks to use their resources to the maximum. Although they would lose interest should rates fall, this was compensated by the fact that call money usually cost slightly more than time money and was, for the most part, the highest rate obtainable in the market. In addition, when rates rose, the banks could easily take advantage of the new opportunities for profits. During the winter of 1919, when speculation was rife and demand high, the call rate [2] hit 30 per cent, providing a windfall for the banks at the expense of speculators. By that time—according to contemporary estimates—the call money market provided some $1 billion for securities purchases.

The time borrower was affected by the rise in the rediscount rate in 1919–1920, but the speculator who had call loans was often crushed. Each time the rediscount rate rose ¼ of 1 per cent, the call money market would fluctuate wildly, leading to liquidations, securities dumping, and downward moves in securities prices. Similarly, a small decline in the rediscount rate would be magnified in the call money market, encourage borrowing, and lead to a rise in prices. Obviously, the bulls [3] on Wall Street strongly supported low interest rates, a low rediscount rate, and any other policy which would result in easy money. The experience of 1920, and the indications that the Federal Reserve would hereafter subscribe to a policy of easy money, were greeted approvingly by the bulls and helped spark a sizable rally late in the year.

This is not to say that there were no dangers in such practices. Should a non-dividend paying stock fail to rise, then the buyer would have a loss equal to the interest charges. More

2. The *call rate* is the rate at which call money may be obtained. Thus, 30 per cent call indicates that banks and brokers demand 30 per cent interest on these loans.

3. *Bulls* are those who are optimistic as to future moves on the Exchange and elsewhere. Accordingly, they will buy stocks, and their activities will tend to lift prices higher.

serious, however, were the risks of a bear market. Once the security's price fell below a certain point, the borrower might be asked by his broker to provide "more margin," or collateral. For example, an individual might purchase $100 worth of stock on 90 per cent margin, putting up the stock as collateral. Should the stock's value fall to $90, his investment would be wiped out. When the price fell below $90, the purchaser would be asked to provide more collateral. Should he fail to do this, the bank would be empowered to sell the securities at the market, recovering whatever it could from the loan. Naturally, the higher the percentage of the loan, the more chance there was for a call. This is why those who purchased stock with time loans of 50 per cent were considered investors in 1920 while those who bought stocks for 90 per cent call through a loan arranged by a broker were considered speculators. In the sharp decline of 1919–1920, many speculators were wiped out by calls for more margin which could not be met, but few who used time loans were so affected. On the other hand, the speculators made much larger profits in recovery periods. The lesson was clear and simple: in bear markets, all purchases should be on low margin, while bull market buyers should try to get the highest margin available. It was little wonder, then, that the reliance upon call money expanded greatly in the period following the 1920 market lows, and that as the market continued its advance and confidence grew, demands for call money increased.

The mainstays of the financial community—men associated with J. P. Morgan & Co., Kuhn, Loeb & Co., or the major banks—frowned on those speculators who frequented the call money market, despite the fact that they made loans to them when conditions warranted. The large institutions were care-takers of what was called "the Wall Street Point of View." For the most part they were Republican in politics, Protestant in religion (with the notable exception of the Goldman, Sachs and Kuhn, Loeb groups, who were German Jews), and Victorian in their public morality. They were interested in civic improvement, the arts, and "deserving charities." Wall Street's inner circle was intensely patriotic, but also viewed America as part of an Atlantic civilization grounded in the British Isles. Financial leaders admired and preferred presidents like Grover Cleveland and William McKinley, accepted Theodore Roosevelt, and had contempt and fear for Woodrow Wilson and William Jennings Bryan, whom they considered reactionary provincials who would destroy the business fabric if given the opportunity. Their favorite philosopher was Herbert Spencer, the apostle of *laissez faire* who had indicated years earlier that businessmen were indeed the fittest of the community. Writing in 1921, Sereno Pratt, one of the Establishment himself, said:

The broker is usually a gentleman and dresses well and lives well. Sometimes he is something more than a broker, and becomes a power outside of his own class. Brayton Ives, a former President of the Exchange, became a noted collector of books. Another President, A. S. Hatch, was a well-known worker in church missions. Still another President, J. Edward Simmons, was President of the Board of Education and later of the Chamber of Commerce. Another President, James D. Smith, was Commodore of the New York Yacht Club. S. V. White, besides being a broker, was a member of the bar of the Supreme Court, and served in Congress. Stedman was a poet. R. P. Flower was Governor of the State. Bird S. Coler served as Comptroller of the city. On the whole, brokers as a class compare well, mentally and morally, with other business men. They are always patriotic, if for no other motive than that of self-interest, for if the Government went down or suffered from domestic revolt or foreign invasion, the whole structure of Wall Street credits and values would collapse like a house of cards. During the Civil War the Exchange would not admit as member anyone suspected of aiding in the rebellion. The broker is proverbially generous. When he makes money, he spends it freely, and his contributions to charity are liberal.[4]

Members of the Exchange usually came from the same upper class social group, went to the correct prep schools, and then on to Harvard, Yale, or Princeton. Despite their advantages and the inbreeding which continually took place among them,

4. Sereno Pratt. *The Work of Wall Street* (New York, 1920), p. 216.

the leaders of Wall Street still preached the gospel of work in 1920. "The trouble with Harvard University," said businessman Robert Bradley, "is that a man is not taught to do anything thoroughly." Another observed that Marshall Field & Co., the large department store, had 40,000 employees, "and there is not a university man in the whole establishment except fifth down the line. You get your men of the future from the office boys and the young men who come into your office." [5] Such individuals might hope for clerks' positions on Wall Street, or might—if extremely talented—aspire to the post of floor trader.[6] But the inner circle, which included membership in the New York Stock Exchange, was closed. True, an ambitious young man might be able to purchase a seat, and through good fortune make his mark on the community. But the rarefied air was controlled by Morgan & Co. and a few others, and doors were closed to any upstart who might take the rags to riches story seriously.

Although the New York Stock Exchange dominated trading in the financial district, it was not the only market for securities in the city. The Consolidated Stock Exchange, formed in 1886, still did a small amount of business but, since most of its shares were also listed on the Big Board, it declined throughout the period. The Curb Exchange,[7] specializing in newer companies' shares and low-priced issues in general, had more listings, and the over-the-counter market of unlisted stocks was large and

5. Clarence Barron. *They Told Barron* (New York, 1930), pp. 94–95, 298.

6. A *floor trader* is an Exchange member whose function it is to buy and sell securities on the floor of the Exchange. Such individuals are key men in any brokerage firm.

7. The *Curb Exchange* was a leading securities market, second only to the New York Stock Exchange (also called "The Big Board") in total volume for an organized exchange. Operations were held in the open, at Wall and Hanover streets, and, later on, on Broad Street below Exchange Place. Its name was derived from the fact that most trades were actually made at the street curb. The Curb Exchange moved indoors to offices at 86 Trinity Place in 1921, but retained its old name until 1953 when it was changed to American Stock Exchange.

nebulous. It is difficult to say just how many shares were traded at the smaller markets in 1920 since they did not publish figures regularly. As for the New York Stock Exchange, there were few million-share days that year. On a normal trading session, 600,000–800,000 shares would change hands, of the approximately 250 million shares listed. In the previous year 318 million shares were traded for a turnover rate of 153 per cent, a figure which has not been surpassed since. In contrast, 10-million-share days were not unusual in 1968.

As in the past, there were two types of stock issues in 1920—common and preferred. Preferred stock received a fixed dividend, but had no voting rights. The common received irregular dividends, but could vote for the firm's management. Before the war investors generally dealt in preferred stocks, which yielded 6–8 per cent in many cases for high-grade issues and showed few fluctuations. Common stocks could move rapidly since in good years they would receive high dividends, but in bad ones perhaps none at all. As a result, common stock appealed to speculators and those interested in accumulating sufficient shares to take over an enterprise.

Before the war, most large corporations considered earnings after taxes and payments to bondholders and preferred stockholders a "surplus," and much of this was divided among the common stockholders. This meant that such firms would have to depend heavily upon the capital markets for funds needed for expansion, and large bond issues were considered normal.

A new philosophy of financing emerged during the war, borrowed in part from the experience of utility companies. These firms would pay interest on bonds and dividends to preferred stockholders, and then set aside sizable portions of the surplus in various funds, some to amortize equipment, others for future expansion. Only part of what was left was disbursed to common stockholders. As a result, the utilities were able to plan their financing with greater care. Although stockholders did not receive all the surplus, they were compensated by being paid regular dividends instead of the usual windfalls once or twice a year.

By 1922, many large industrial firms were on a regular dividend-paying basis, retaining large portions of earnings in the form of special funds. The public accepted this innovation, especially when the regular dividends were increased from time

Range and Dividends for Selected Common Stocks, 1921[8]

STOCK	HIGH	LOW	DIVIDEND
Allied Chemical & Dye	59¼	34	$ 4.00
American Can	35½	23½	—
American Smelting & Refining	47¼	29⅝	—
American Sugar Refining	96	47⅝	—
American Tobacco "B"	131½	110	12.00
Bethlehem Steel	62½	39½	5.00
General Electric	143¾	109½	12.00
General Motors	16¼	9⅜	1.00
Goodrich	44⅛	26⅝	—
International Harvester	100½	67⅝	5.00
International Nickel	17	11½	—
North American	46	32¼	3.00
Sears Roebuck	98¾	54¼	—
Standard Oil of New Jersey	192¼	124½	5.00
Texas Company	48	29	3.00
Texas Gulf Sulphur	42	32⅝	2.50
United States Steel	86½	70¼	5.00
Westinghouse E & M	52¼	38⅞	4.00
Woolworth, F. W.	136¾	105	8.00
Wright Aeronautical	9⅝	6½	1.00

SOURCE: *New York Times,* December 31, 1921.

8. Tables such as these are familiar to Wall Streeters, and will be used to illustrate trading throughout this book. *Stock* refers to the common stock of a firm. In the case of American Tobacco, there were two classes of common stock, "A" and "B," of which "B" was the more actively traded. *High* refers to the highest purchase price for the time period involved, and *Low* to the lowest. Thus, at one point in 1921, Allied Chemical & Dye traded shares at 59¼, while at another it sold for 34. All these figures refer to dollars. Thus, had you purchased Allied Chemical & Dye at its high, it would have cost you $59.25. *Dividends* are shares of the profits of a company distributed to stockholders.

to time. In addition, these firms would rarely cut their payments. If short of liquid assets and unwilling to go to the capital markets to borrow money, the firm would issue stock in lieu of cash. In effect, a firm might distribute 1/10th of a share of stock with a par value [9] of $100 in place of a $10 dividend; this too was accepted by shareholders, especially in a rising market. These stock dividends gained an added appeal when in April of 1920 the Supreme Court declared them exempt from income taxes.

Finally, firms began to raise money through direct offerings to shareholders rather than by using the capital markets. Owners of common stock would be given the right to purchase additional shares at a price slightly lower than that quoted on Wall Street. This method was particularly attractive when prices were considered too high by the banking community, which might refuse loans at what the firm thought reasonable rates. Since rights would increase in value when the stocks rose, the shareholder considered them more valuable than extra dividends, and began to look forward to them.

This new philosophy of finance served to make common stocks more attractive than preferred issues. Stock dividends, rights, and dividend increases were shared by the common, not preferred stockholders. The main advantage preferred had over common, that of stability of return, was now gone, since regular payments to common stockholders were initiated. As a result,

9. *Par value* had meaning at one time, but by the 1920s it was no longer considered of great importance. A century earlier it referred to the original value of shares of common stock, and the amount for which the holder was liable. Thus, a share with a par value of $100 might be sold for $80 by the company, with the understanding that it could call upon the holder for the additional $20 whenever necessary. Dividends were distributed in terms of par value; if a company's common shares had a par value of $100, and it declared a 6 per cent dividend, this would mean that each shareholder received $6.00 per share. Finally, par value had meaning for the firm's accountants. A firm with 1 million shares of common stock outstanding, each with a par value of $10, would have an item of $10 million on the debit side of its balance sheet. Par value has no true meaning today, and most corporations are tending to abandon the concept.

more people attempted to purchase common stocks than ever before, and this served as a major support for the market rise which began after the postwar depression.

As important as this innovation was to stockholders, it held greater implications for the economy as a whole, especially when viewed in the context of other developments. As a result of America's pre-eminent position in the postwar world, corporations were situated to make more profits than ever before. Friendly administrations in Washington would do little to hamper their expansion. These profits would not be disbursed, but instead used to expand the enterprises and provide for still greater growth in the future. Whatever money could not be gained through internal financing might be borrowed at low rates, made possible by the easy money policy of the Federal Reserve. The economic growth would be reflected in higher prices on Wall Street, and the increases would attract new money to the securities exchanges. In time the Establishment— the men who held to the Wall Street Point of View—would be replaced by newcomers, more in tune with the new spirit. This vision and analysis would become the text for many speeches by business and government leaders from 1921 to 1928. They could, with reason, observe that theirs was the greatest growth period in American history, a time of qualitative and quantitative change. Optimism seemed justified, and so the bull market which began in 1921 did not appear unreasonable to those who participated. Flaws were seen by a few, but these were minor points when set alongside the great gains of this unusual era.

2

An Age of
Innovation and Growth

THE Committee on Recent Economic Changes, established by President Hoover's Conference on Unemployment, published its final report in the spring of 1929. The Committee attempted to explain the rapid and apparently solid growth which had taken place since 1921. "Acceleration, rather than structural change, is the key to an understanding of our recent economic development," was its conclusion. The Committee observed that no major new product had appeared since the end of the war. When asked to list the most important discoveries of the decade, businessmen mentioned cellophane, celluloid, antifreeze, oleomargarine, bakelite, and rayon. All made their impressions, but none were vital to the economy of the twenties.

More important were the figures on the growth of power. While the population increased 62 per cent from 1899 to 1929, and wage earners 88 per cent, production rose 295 per cent and electric power generation by 331 per cent. The *per capita* production of the American worker was 60 per cent higher in 1929 than it had been thirty years earlier. In 1919 32 per cent of factory machinery was powered by electricity; by 1929 the figure was 49 per cent. During the decade the number of kilowatt hours *per capita* rose from 410 to 774. By 1929, the United States was producing more electric power than the rest of the world combined.

The application of this power in old industries, internal reorganizations within the industries, rapid expansion of foreign markets, and, most important, the introduction of new techniques of marketing and mass distribution, helped make the twenties an era of growth and gave the decade its glow of prosperity. This aspect of the twenties, at least, was not tinsel, but substantial in almost every respect. During the decade American business added $100 billion in new capital equipment, loaned an additional $10 billion to foreign nations, and paid off $7 billion of the national debt, and all of this was accomplished without inflation.[1]

Industrial reorganization, combination, and consolidation, together with a wave of merger activity, marked the business scene in the twenties. The origins of these movements are obscure, but certainly they were aided by the need for efficiency during the war and the suspension of antitrust actions. In 1920 the Supreme Court declared, by a 4–3 vote, that U. S. Steel need not be dissolved. Although the firm had attempted to monopolize the industry, it had failed to do so, and therefore could remain intact. The Justice Department indicated a willingness to allow further combinations in steel, so long as the industry leader was not involved. In the following nine years Bethlehem absorbed Lackawanna, Midvale, Cambria, Pacific Coast, and Southern California. Weirton, Great Lakes, and M. A. Hanna combined to form National Steel, and Republic added Central Alloy, Donner, and Bourne Fuller. By 1929 the industry was dominated by a half dozen giant holding companies that set prices through the medium of a trade association, which the Supreme Court did not consider a combination in restraint of trade. In the Cement Manufacturers Protective Association case and the Maple Flooring Manufacturers Association case the Court reiterated this opinion. Finally, in 1924, the Justice Department dropped its action against Aluminum Company of America, which had been charged with having a monopoly position in the metal. It was clear that as far as the Attorney General was concerned, the Sherman and Clayton Antitrust Acts were dead letters. Big businessmen joined in

1. See Appendix.

protective associations and smaller ones in chambers of commerce. All were dedicated to the belief that competition was wasteful and that through cooperation costs could be lowered, prices stabilized, and profits enhanced.

Other industries mirrored the changes made in steel. In automobiles, Alfred Sloan's program of decentralization at General Motors helped make that firm the leader of the industry. Henry Ford was still admired, but the age of rugged individualism was gone, to be replaced by that of the smooth working business team. Ford's unwillingness to delegate authority, together with his insistence that Americans wanted basic transportation—and nothing else—from their cars almost wrecked his company. In motion pictures, several large firms—Famous-Players-Lasky, R.K.O., and Paramount—came to dominate the industry after a period of monopoly followed by one of cutthroat competition. A similar situation existed in radio, as networks were organized by Westinghouse, American Telephone & Telegraph, and others. By the end of the decade, oligopoly,[2] industrial cooperation, and stability—together with growth—were the hallmarks of most major industries. In addition, the large corporation became even more powerful and ubiquitous than it had been earlier. As late as 1923, the 1,240 largest manufacturing firms sold 69.4 per cent of goods produced by American corporations. By 1929—when more than 92 per cent of all goods were products of corporations—the 1,289 largest accounted for 75.6 per cent of them. Profits were high, and the size of the firms indicated a certain stability. There was every reason to hope for still greater profits, and to believe that new industries would grow rapidly. And these beliefs were quickly transformed into higher prices on the New York Stock Exchange and other markets.

The most dramatic example of this optimism was the case of Radio Corporation of America, which was formed through a reorganization in 1919. During the twenties RCA was in-

2. *Oligopoly* refers to control of an industry or product by a limited number of companies.

volved in several glamour industries—set manufacture, stations, motion pictures, and so forth—and the firm caught the public's fancy. In 1921, RCA stock traded over-the-counter [3] for as low as 1½. Then it began to rise.

Yearly Price Range for
Radio Corporation of America Common Stock

YEAR	HIGH	LOW
1921	2½	1½
1922	6¼	2⅛
1923	4¾	2¾
1924	66⅞	42⅛ *
1925	77⅞	39¼
1926	61⅝	32
1927	101	41⅛
1928	420	85¼
1929	114¾	26 **

* After reorganization, including the issuance of one share of new common for five of the old stock.
** After a stock split of five for one.
SOURCE: *Poor's Industrial Section,* 1930 (New York, 1930), p. 2883.

Given Europe's shattered economies and the rapid growth in America, it was only natural that the nation's business leaders would look overseas for additional customers. By the end of the decade, Americans had replaced the British in many Latin American markets, and were exporting more to Asia and Europe than ever before. At the same time, due to the passage of high tariffs by Congress and their approval by the executive branch, Europeans were unable to compete successfully in American markets. The result was a "favorable balance of trade" throughout the decade. From 1922 to 1929, American exports rose

3. The *over-the-counter* market, then and now, is the largest market in the United States, though it is disorganized and held together by telephone wires alone. All stocks not listed on an exchange, as well as government bonds, most bank and insurance securities, and other unlisted securities, are bought and sold here. Ordinarily, new firms or small companies will apply for listing on an exchange when and if they meet the qualifications. Thus, RCA traded over-the-counter at first, and later on applied for and received listing on the New York Stock Exchange.

26 per cent and imports only 16 per cent. In 1929 Americans exported $5.24 billion worth of goods—a peacetime record. That same year the nation imported $4.4 billion in goods, a figure which was less than 1926's $4.43 billion and below prewar levels.

In a few cases these imports were paid for with gold shipments, but most of the time Europe and Latin America attempted to borrow from Americans or were obliged to accept American investments in local industries. In 1919 Americans owned $6.9 billion worth of foreign securities and promissory notes; the figure was $17 billion in mid-1929. Before the war direct investments overseas were little more than $1.8 billion; by 1929 they were $7.47 billion. General Motors alone invested some $50 million overseas in the twenties, and other firms followed close behind.

If foreigners needed dollars to purchase American goods, then American firms were eager to find new areas for investment of their surpluses. As profits grew and domestic investment leveled off, foreign fields seemed most attractive, especially when overseas interest rates were high. In every year but one from 1919 to 1929, the dollar amounts of new foreign securities floated in America increased. Between 1925 and 1929 alone, $5.1 billion in loans were gained in America.

Some 36 houses, most of them American, competed for a city of Budapest loan and 14 for a loan to the city of Belgrade. A Bavarian hamlet, discovered by American agents to be in need of about $125,000, was urged and finally persuaded to borrow $3 million in the American market. In Peru, a group of successful American promoters included one Peruvian, the son of the President of that republic, who was afterwards tried by the courts of his country and convicted of "illegal enrichment." In Cuba the son-in-law of the President was given a well-paid position in the Cuban branch of an American bank during most of the time the bank was successfully competing against other American banks for the privilege of financing the Cuban government.[4]

4. Cleona Lewis. *America's Stake in International Investments* (Washington, 1938), p. 377.

Large-scale loans were granted to Latin American countries throughout the decade. American banks floated several German bond issues, and the Germans used part of the money to pay war reparations to Britain and France, who in turn sent the money back to America in payment of war loans, completing the cycle. The end result of all these manipulations and flotations was to make America the world's banker, and to replace London with New York as its money capital. Insofar as the stock markets were concerned, promises of overseas bonanzas spurred prices onward, and increased earnings of companies with foreign affiliates led their stocks into new high ground toward the end of the decade.

More important than the foreign markets, however, was the growth in America of what came to be called "consumerism." Before the war, credit for consumers' goods was granted, but not exploited. For the most part, the would-be purchaser of an appliance or home improvement believed he would need cash before entering a store. One of the reasons Henry Ford struggled to bring down the price of his Model "T" was to enable millions who otherwise could not afford an automobile to purchase one. But Ford was unwilling to base his sales campaign on credit; although dealers would sell on time, they were discouraged from doing so by the factory.

Similarly, advertising was still in its infancy in 1914. Department stores, national branded goods, and some local products took out advertisements in newspapers, and billboards were common sights, but most appeals were crude, unimaginative, sober, and ill conceived. What was needed at this time was a concerted campaign, deployed through the proper media, and tied to credit purchases. All three came together in the early twenties.

The possibilities of consumerism were obvious to many businessmen before the war. The nation was in a recession in 1913, with attendant unemployment and closed factories. Millions of Americans were without many of the basic necessities of life, not to mention what at the time seemed luxuries, such as indoor plumbing and electrification. It was clear, even then, that the nation's factories were capable of turning out goods that would raise the living standard dramatically, but that potential consumers lacked the wherewithal to purchase these goods. As late as 1920 there were only thirteen bathtubs and six telephones for every hundred people in the nation's cities, and the figures were lower for the farm population. Although one family in three had an automobile, less than one in 10,000 owned a radio. One out of every ten city dwellings was electrified; almost no farms had electricity. Should wires be brought to these homes, their owners would become customers for the great variety of appliances then being offered. If radios and indoor plumbing could be purchased with low initial payments, then millions might avail themselves of these "innovations."

With the return of prosperity and the rapid expansion of the economy following the postwar depression, many firms began to mount large-scale advertising campaigns tied to credit buying. Bruce Barton, a pioneer of modern advertising and one of the prophets of the period, intuitively recognized that this was the key to increased sales, higher profits, and a better standard of living. In 1924 he attempted to give selling a moral flavor as well. In that year he reflected on his lack of interest as a youth in the Bible. This was because he was repelled by the image of Jesus most writers offered. But then, according to Barton, he reread the book and realized that Jesus was not a weakling, a dreamer, or a person interested only in other-worldly affairs. Instead, He was a man who "picked up twelve men from the bottom ranks of business and forged them into an organization that conquered the world."

Some day . . . some one will write a book about Jesus. Every business man will read it and send it to his partners and his sales-men. For it will tell the story of the founder of modern business.[5]

Barton wrote the book himself, *The Man Nobody Knows,* and it became the bestselling work of the year. Business was

5. Bruce Barton. *The Man Nobody Knows* (New York, 1924), pp. iii–iv.

moral, selling was akin to prayer, and God meant us to enjoy ourselves on Earth, was his message. *The Man Nobody Knows* did not mould the decade's atmosphere, but did reflect the changes Barton and his followers were bringing to the marketplace. Three years later Wesley C. Mitchell, one of the nation's leading economists, put matters in a more scholarly context.

Yet with all their puzzles, consumers are in a strong market position. Their formal freedom to spend their money incomes as they like, combined with their massive inertia, keeps producers under pressur⌐ to solicit customers, to teach the public to want more goods and new goods. This task of stimulating demand is never done; for the march of technological improvement is ever increasing our capacity to produce, and before we have learned to distribute and to use what has just been added to our output, new advances have been scored. Hence the chronic complaint of businessmen that our industries are "over built." [6]

What both men were saying, in effect, was that the new era of American capitalism had seen an end in many fields of competition in prices and variety of products; it was one in which firms and products would compete on the basis of advertisements, credit, and services. Mitchell's businessmen were concerned about rapid technological change, but this was not their major problem. Nor were industries "over built" in 1927. Instead the factories, stimulated by the growth of consumerism earlier in the decade, were on the verge of overproducing after a generation of underproducing.

Consumerism was stoked by large infusions of advertising capital. Figures on these expenses were not calculated before the war, but estimates vary between $350 million and $400 million. In contrast, $1.5 billion was spent on advertising in 1927. The largest amount—$690 million—went to newspapers. Another $210 million was spent on magazines, and $75 million on billboards. Only $7 million was spent for radio advertisements that year, but this was the fastest growing segment of

6. Wesley C. Mitchell. *Business Cycles: The Problem and Its Setting* (New York, 1927), p. 166.

the industry. Direct mailings and announcements accounted for some $400 million, with the rest distributed to trade journals, streetcar signs, and other media. And still the field expanded. By 1929, more than $1.8 billion was being spent on advertising.

Consumer goods which might be purchased on time accounted for the bulk of the new advertisements. For example, magazine ads for radios rose from less than $80,000 in 1922 to $3.4 million in 1927. There were few advertisements for electric refrigerators in 1922; by 1927 more than $1.5 million was spent to advertise them. Automobiles, which accounted for less than 10 per cent of newspaper ads in 1922, rose to 19.3 per cent in 1927. And other consumer durables were not far behind.

In addition to formal ads, the new communications media made possible more subtle enticements to buy. As we have seen, the Wall Street Establishment professed to admire men who were willing to start at the bottom of the ladder and work their way up. This Horatio Alger–Social Darwinist morality was countered by a new variety in the motion pictures of the twenties. In many of them, viewers saw their favorite stars consuming goods—at parties, on yachts, in plush apartments— but rarely were screenplays written to show how they earned their money. Motion picture heroes and heroines were pre-eminently consumers of luxury items, not producers of the necessities of life. One could hardly expect viewers to accept Rudolph Valentino in the role of a poor clerk who struggled to make his mark, or Gloria Swanson as an urban housewife trying to stretch her budget. Instead they dressed well, rode in expensive cars, and lived in sumptuous surroundings. Their fans, watching such lives at the nickelodeons, were often tempted to emulate them. More than books or radio, the motion pictures set the style for aspiring individuals in the twenties.

Such people could hardly afford the "good life" on their salaries, but with the aid of time payments, they could own some of the items seen in advertisements and movies. Credit sales rose rapidly during the twenties, especially in the field

of consumer durables. By 1927, 15 per cent of all such goods
—some $6 billion in value—were bought through installment
contracts. Over 85 per cent of all furniture sales, 80 per cent
of phonographs, 75 per cent of washing machines, and more
than half the sales of radios, pianos, sewing machines, vacuum
cleaners, and refrigerators were made this way. The automobile
industry was able to expand production from 1.5 million units
in 1921 to 3.6 million in 1925 through the use of time payments. By 1926 more than 65 per cent of all new and used
cars—over $3 billion in value—were taken after deposits of
small down payments. The new owner received his auto, plus
a coupon book for payments that ran from twenty-four to
thirty-six months. Like advertising, this area of the economy
showed great growth. By 1929, more than $7 billion worth
of consumers' goods were purchased on time.

The economy's ability to absorb these products in such
quantities necessitated rapid expansion of manufacturing, service, and sales facilities. From 1904 to 1913, a yearly average
of $6 billion was spent on new plant and equipment. In 1922
the figure was $11.6 billion and in 1923, $16.7 billion. A
high was reached in 1926—$18 billion—followed by a leveling
off to $16.5 billion in 1929, still a respectable figure. These
statistics were translated into more jobs and purchasing power.
Consumer expenditures, which stood at $56.2 billion in 1922,
reached a new high of $74.3 billion in 1929. Part of this rise
was due to a larger labor force and higher wages, but a significant amount came from the use of consumer credit.

To some commentators, this upward spiral seemed sound
and never-ending. If America had to solve the problem of
distribution, what better way could be found than consumer
credit, which created work and enabled purchasers to enjoy
goods now rather than in the distant future? Others, however,
were concerned with the negative aspects of time payments.
In the first place, the innovation could only have a "one-shot"
impact; an individual could mortgage his salary only once. In
other words, when a consumer's salary was completely com-

mitted to the purchase of necessities plus time payments, he
was effectively out of the market. Secondly, such a person
would be at the mercy of the economy. Should he miss a few
weeks' pay, he would not be able to meet his payments, at
which point the goods purchased on time might be repossessed.
Finally, what would happen in a period of recession? In 1927
the president of Studebaker Corporation, noting that almost
$1.5 billion in unpaid installment notes were outstanding for
his industry, asked, "What would occur should there be another
1893?" Should such a panic and depression hit, the department stores would be inundated with a flood of repossessed
goods for which there would be no market, and the automobile
companies would have to take back hundreds of thousands of
cars, with no buyers for them. Since most finance companies
were intimately connected with the banks, such a situation could
easily cause several major failures, which would spread throughout the economy and lead to financial chaos. But this did not
materialize during the two recessionary years of the decade—
1924 and 1927—and by 1929 such disasters were no longer
considered seriously.

For the short run at least, consumer credit combined with
other previously discussed aspects of the economy to produce
higher earnings for many corporations. Ordinarily, stock prices
would rise at the same rate as earnings. But by the middle
of the decade, securities salesmen were telling potential customers that buying stocks on margin was no different than paying
for a radio on time. In fact, such a commitment made more
sense than a new radio in the parlor. The purchaser of a
receiving set would pay for an item which remained constant in
value or, as was more often the case, depreciated. A share of
RCA common stock might double in less time than it took
to pay off the note. The set purchaser of 1926 could put down
$10 for a $50 table model and pay off the note in twelve
months, at which time he would be the owner of a used
receiver which had cost him $60 or so after charges were
added, but which was worth less than $25 on the used radio

market. On the other hand, a $10 bill used to buy one share of RCA on 90 per cent margin would bring the speculator a $100 profit should the stock rise from $100 to $200. And with some of the increment, the happy speculator could buy his set—or several of them—on time.

Such blandishments won many small plungers for the securities markets. Throughout the decade, and especially after 1927, the stock exchanges were flooded with individuals who had no previous experience in buying and selling securities. By then the dream of great wealth and of a limitless bull market seemed more real than fanciful.

In this period several analysts—Wesley Mitchell and *The New York Times* financial editor Alexander Dana Noyes among them—warned of soft spots in the economy. While admitting that aggregate figures offered a powerful argument for prosperity, Mitchell was concerned about weaknesses in coal mining and textiles, where unemployment grew due to the development of new power sources and an oversupply of cotton. The South as a region did not share in the prosperity. Although farm income rose, the farmer lagged behind the rest of the nation in the twenties. Most important, industrial wages did not reflect the great gains made in productivity. Although real wages rose in the early part of the decade, they stagnated from 1923 to 1925, rose slightly in 1926, and then leveled off once again. From 1918 to 1928, real wages rose 26 per cent. In this same period, productivity climbed 40 per cent. The meaning of these figures was simple: the worker was producing more than ever before, but was not receiving a proportionate share of his increased productivity. This was retained by the corporations and was reflected in better earnings statements, which in turn led to higher prices on the stock exchanges.

Such a situation could not last indefinitely. For a while consumer credit could compensate for the lag in wages. When the purchasers were fully committed and could no longer buy on time, the sales figures would inevitably decline. American workers were producing more goods, but they lacked the where-withal to buy them as consumers. Weak unions, pro-business governments, and a triumphant business community gave the decade the aura of prosperity, and led securities prices to higher levels. But in the end, the fatal flaw of low wages in an economy of high productivity would haunt the nation.

3

The Business of Government

THE POLITICAL SCENE of the twenties was as crowded as any in the nation's history, but none was as bereft of new talent and ideas. Prominent statesmen like Robert La Follette, William McAdoo, William Borah, Hiram Johnson, George Norris and Charles Evans Hughes were relics of progressivism and World War I, and they continued to play important roles in the twenties. But the new men of the decade—people who made their impact on the national scene—were, for the most part, second raters. Smith Brookhart, James Cox, John W. Davis, Charles Dawes, Albert Ritchie, Gilbert Haughen, Reed Smoot, Frank Lowden, and Owen Young—all appeared significant individuals at one time or another during the twenties, but none survived into the next decade. Here and there one could find a Fiorello La Guardia, a Burton Wheeler, or a Robert La Follette, Jr., but their numbers were small compared to the great talents of the prewar years and what would follow in the thirties. Even Al Smith, that singular figure who spanned both eras, was on the scrap heap by 1933. The men of the twenties represent a "lost generation" in more ways than are usually meant.

This is not to say that prominent statesmen and politicians of the period lacked power and talent, but merely that they refused to use them. They attempted to return the nation to an imagined pre-progressive utopia rather than responding to the problems of the decade. While the businessman saw a vision of a cooperative capitalist society marked by consumerism

and ever-increasing profits, political leaders longed for the pre–
Theodore Roosevelt era of benign government, isolationism,
and the virtues of small-town America. Interestingly enough,
the two attitudes worked well together, enabling business to
expand without government interference, high taxes, or fears
of control.

This could be seen in the philosophies and statements of
the Presidents of the decade. In his inaugural address, Warren
Harding enunciated his view that there should be "less government in business and more business in government." His successor, Calvin Coolidge, said on several occasions that "the
business of America is business." Herbert Hoover, easily the
most capable statesman of the three, spoke of the "New Era"
in which cooperation in business, aided by government and
guided by scientific principles, would lead to prosperity for
the nation and greater freedom in all aspects of life. Such
statements supported by actions—and the lack of them—gave
business confidence in Washington, the businessman a new
status in his community, and fostered the air of optimism on
Wall Street.

Throughout the twenties, national political power was held
by men who rejected the basic assumptions of the progressives
and the visions of Wilsonian internationalists. National administrations did not consider big business an evil, refused to distin-
guish between good and bad trusts, tried to limit rather than
expand their scope of power, and attempted to keep the peace
through a policy of issuing statements of intent and signing
nonenforceable treaties, while maintaining the nation aloof
from the League of Nations. In effect, the national administrations desired to return to the period of the late nineteenth
century, without the depressed business conditions of the time,
with New York rather than London at the center of world
finance, and with America, rather than Great Britain, maintaining splendid isolation by fostering a balance of power on the
continent. A return to the gold standard was imperative, as
were payments of debts and the meeting of other international

obligations. No administration of the decade attempted to stray far from these objectives.

Monetary and fiscal policies were essential tools in achieving these goals. Most businessmen wanted an end to talk of graduated taxes, lower tax rates in general, a budgetary surplus so as to pay off the national debt, and a favorable balance of trade. Three Republican administrations worked toward these ends. Furthermore, the business community wanted low interest rates and a plentiful money supply. This was made possible by Federal Reserve policies after the depression of 1920–1921.

Presidents Harding and Coolidge were content to allow matters of fiscal policy to be decided by Andrew Mellon, called in the twenties "the greatest Treasury Secretary since Alexander Hamilton." Mellon was one of the three or four most influential men in the government; it was said later that "three presidents served under him." The head of the powerful Pittsburgh clan— influential in aluminum, banking, petroleum, and other aspects of business as well as one of the richest men in the world— Mellon could scarcely be expected to do anything business opposed. The Treasury Secretary cut expenditures for almost every department of government, especially those which had regulatory functions. For example, the Interior Department, which was given $48.8 million in 1921, received $32.8 million in 1928. On the other hand, the Commerce Department, which under Secretary Hoover worked so as to aid business, saw its budget rise from $25.9 million to $34.4 million in the same period. In addition to lowering expenditures, Mellon showed surpluses every year of the decade, paid off a substantial portion of the national debt, and provided an atmosphere of stability which Wall Street appreciated. "The Government is just a business, and can and should be run on business principles," he said. And so he did.

Throughout the decade, Mellon fought off those who would spend more on bonuses, public works projects, and public services. Together with the State and War departments, the Treasury attempted successfully to hold down expenditures on armaments.

Federal Receipts, Expenditures, and Debts (in millions)

YEAR	RECEIPTS	EXPENDI-TURES	SURPLUS	TOTAL DEBT
1920	$6,705	$6,220	$484	$24,299
1921	5,585	4,896	689	23,977
1922	4,104	3,618	485	22,963
1923	3,847	3,648	199	22,350
1924	3,884	3,404	480	21,251
1925	3,608	2,931	677	20,516
1926	3,908	3,518	391	19,643
1927	4,024	3,417	607	18,512
1928	4,038	3,647	391	17,604
1929	4,036	3,852	184	16,931

SOURCE: *Annual Reports of the Secretary of the Treasury, 1920–1930.*

Having accomplished these operations, Mellon was able to pay off a substantial part of the debt and at the same time cut taxes.

The Secretary felt it immoral for the government to tax heavily, directly, and on a graduated basis. While he could scarcely repeal the tax laws, he could change them so as to lower rates, especially for those Mellon felt made the nation vital: the very rich. By the end of the decade, the 60,000 families at the top of the economy were worth as much as the 25 million at the bottom. It was these 60,000 that Mellon worked to assist.

In 1921 Mellon was able to push a tax reduction through Congress. Under its terms, the wartime excess profits tax was repealed, the corporation tax was lowered to 2½ per cent, the maximum personal income tax was reduced from 65 to 32 per cent, and several luxury taxes were done away with entirely. In order to win Democrats such as Carter Glass and John Nance Garner to his program, Mellon also raised the exemption for the head of a family from $2,000 to $2,500, and reduced taxes on lower incomes as well. Still, the major beneficiaries of the 1921 act were wealthy individuals and large corporations. Other tax cuts came in 1924, 1926, and 1928, all compromises, and all serving to aid business and the rich.

Mellon's friends argued that those whose incomes exceeded $100,000 paid a larger proportion of the total tax bill in 1929 than they had in 1920, while taxes for those with incomes under $5,000 were almost eliminated. While this was true, it should also be noted that Mellon's new laws made it possible for wealthy individuals to practice tax avoidance with ease; the Secretary put dozens of loopholes into the laws. Later on it was disclosed that Jack Morgan and other prominent bankers and businessmen actually paid no taxes at all during several years of the decade. It was also learned that Secretary Mellon had initiated a generous policy of tax rebates, dispensing $3.5 billion to individuals who had paid too much in taxes earlier. Most of the recipients of such windfalls were or shortly became prominent in Republican fund raising efforts. Nor did the Mellon program fail to benefit the Secretary's own interests. Senator Norris of Nebraska noted that under the terms of one tax bill, "Mr. Mellon himself gets a larger personal reduction than the aggregate of practically all the taxpayers in the state of Nebraska."

There were still several more important effects of the Mellon program. In the first place, it enabled corporations to report higher incomes than might otherwise have been the case. Improved earnings were quickly translated into higher prices for stocks on Wall Street. Secondly, the wealthy upper crust of America now had more money than ever before, and they used a good part of it to purchase securities. Next, the Mellon cuts removed or lowered taxes on capital gains, encouraging individuals and corporations to switch their investments from interest-free state and municipal bonds to common stocks. Finally, the payment of the national debt meant fewer refinancing efforts by the Treasury, and fewer drains on the investment market for funds. As we shall see, the Federal Reserve purchased large quantities of government obligations during most years of the decade, leaving the field of government bills rather barren. What all this meant, in the end, was that corporation earnings reports were increasingly better, and stock prices were higher due to switches from bonds and the presence of more money on Wall Street, while the government bond and bill market tended to stagnate. No wonder, then, that one disgruntled Democrat called Secretary Mellon "the fairy godfather of the bull market."

Mellon's program would have been seriously hindered had not the Federal Reserve philosophy developed along parallel lines. After the 1920–1921 depression and until 1928, the central bank operated with three goals in mind: 1) to encourage domestic business; 2) to prevent inflation while at the same time satisfying congressional critics it would not cause a recession; 3) to maintain international liquidity through cooperation with European banks.

The Federal Reserve Board during the twenties was dominated by men of unusual incompetence and ignorance. Daniel Crissinger, a Harding crony, became Governor of the Board; a small-town attorney and banker, Crissinger stood in awe of the great of New York, knew little of finance and could scarcely follow an argument in economics, and was a poor administrator. Likewise George James, a Memphis banker and merchant, was quite ignorant of central banking issues. Adolph Miller showed flashes of intelligence, but was unable to frame alternative policies. Edward Cunningham was named to the Board in 1923 as the farm bloc's representative. Intelligent and respected, he nonetheless knew little of banking. Edmund Platt of Poughkeepsie, New York, was a political appointee who was content to remain a time server. And so it went with the rest of them. In the end, most reluctantly accepted the leadership of Secretary Mellon, who was an *ex officio* member of the Board. Like Mellon, the majority of Board members came to consider the interests of business paramount in their actions.

In the first years of the decade, the Federal Reserve's major weapon was the rediscount rate. As we have seen, raising and lowering the rate was credited with causing and then correcting the postwar depression. But borrowing did not increase appreciably with low rates in 1922, a fact quickly forgotten by many in the next six years. Instead, the district banks found themselves embarrassed by a cash surplus which member banks would not borrow, since business demand had not yet developed. In the middle of 1922 the member banks began to purchase government obligations with their surpluses, thus gaining short-term investments for themselves while at the same time putting their excess funds into the market. Between October 1921 and May 1922, Federal Reserve banks increased such holdings from $191 million to $603 million. Without realizing it, the System had developed a new tool of monetary control: open market operations. In April 1923 the Open Market Investment Committee was formed, and for the rest of the decade proved as important—and in some cases more important—than the rediscount rate in monetary policy implementation. It meant that through the concerted purchase of government securities, the System could infuse hundreds of millions of dollars into the economy, while sales of securities would dry up investment capital. Open market operations were channeled through New York money markets, while changes in the rediscount rate could affect each member bank directly, obviating the need for New York operations. Thus, a key institutional change in the System worked to aid the Wall Street community in the twenties.

Even had the System desired to exercise power, it lacked the means to do so at that time. The Federal Reserve was still a young and untried institution in the twenties; most leading bankers tended to look upon it as an intrusion Wilsonian tinkerers made possible. While many banks joined the System so as to use its facilities, the bigger ones felt no special loyalty to it, and gave indications of leaving when the situation demanded. In addition, the Federal Reserve Board under Crissinger never had the power its framers thought it would achieve. Instead, the twelve district banks tended to act independently, to the extent of formulating their own rediscount policies. In this regard, the New York bank was often able to lead and control the rest, in large part due to its location at the financial hub of the nation, but also because Benjamin Strong, former ally of the House of Morgan and the dominant banking figure of the decade, was its head.

A product of the New York banking community during its golden age, Strong was a firm believer in the ethic of the international banker, hoped to use his influence to restore stability after the war, and to fit the New York District Bank into the rubric of the old system. It was Strong's conviction that stability could not be restored without international liquidity. France, Great Britain, and Germany—in fact, most of Europe—were exhausted and in bad financial condition. Gold continued to remain in America long after the armistice, and the near insolvency of some nations led to further exports of the metal to New York. Some way had to be found to encourage gold exports to Europe, which would redress the balance and enable the international gold standard to operate once more. Germany's postwar inflation and fears that similar situations would develop elsewhere only aggravated an already tense atmosphere.

Early in the decade, Strong concluded that low bank rates in America and higher ones abroad would attract money to Europe's capitals. Against his instincts, and in cooperation with Montague Norman, the Governor of the Bank of England, and his counterparts in Berlin and Paris, Strong sponsored an easy money policy in America after the postwar recession had ended. In spite of a few attempts to raise rates in order to prevent recession in 1924, Strong remained an easy money advocate for the rest of his life. In 1924, he used open market operations to flood the New York district with cash, and in May and August lowered the rediscount rate from $4\frac{1}{2}$ to 3 per cent. Accordingly, gold exports to America declined and, in early 1925, Britain began importing gold from America once more. By 1925 Strong was able to satisfy his anti-inflationist upbringing by raising the interest rate, this time to $3\frac{1}{2}$ per cent and later to 4 per cent. It appeared that monetary stability had been restored.

At this point Britain threw a bomb into the international arena. Winston Churchill, then Chancellor of the Exchequer, was like Strong, a product of an earlier age. He had dreams of returning to an era when the pound sterling was the world's dominant currency. Britain had been forced to devalue the pound during the war, but in 1925 Churchill took advantage of the seeming stability to restore the old rate, $4.86 to the pound.

The restored rate was more a gesture than a reflection of reality. In fact, it raised the price of Britain's export goods and placed them out of the world market. Once again, gold left England for America and elsewhere, and once again Strong was obliged to lower the rediscount rate. Bowing to pleas from Norman, Reichsbank Governor Hjalmar Schacht, and Charles Rist of the Bank of France, Strong lowered the rate to 3½ per cent in the spring of 1927 and initiated large-scale open market purchases of government securities. Most members of the Federal Reserve Board were silent in the face of this action. Only Adolph Miller, the lone dissenter, protested, calling it "the greatest and boldest operation ever undertaken by the Federal Reserve System," and charging that it "resulted in one of the most costly errors committed by it or any other banking system in the last 75 years."

Miller admitted that Strong's actions in the twenties helped restore international liquidity and, together with American loans, gave the gold standard the appearance of stability. But this façade was purchased at a large price: a tremendous stimulation to the speculative activities on Wall Street.

Easy money meant low bank rates, which in turn meant low-priced call money. Strong and Mellon had hoped that easy money would encourage gold exports to Europe and capital expansion at home, which in fact it did. But, more than that, it increased speculation on Wall Street. Member banks rediscounted at the central bank at low rates, and then loaned the money to brokers who in turn used it to finance stock purchases. At a time when speculation ran rampant on Wall Street, brokers' loans were still available at 5 per cent, the result of the easy money policy practiced in the mid-twenties. In this way, as in many others, well-intentioned actions by government and semigovernment officials enabled the stock market to rise rapidly.

There was still one more political development which aided investors and led to higher prices on Wall Street. In the first years of the decade, most Americans felt uneasy about European affairs. It was evident that conditions had *not* returned to normal. Would the revolution in Russia spread to the rest of Europe? Would Britain and France recover? Would Germany attempt a war of revenge? Such questions were constantly presented to Americans by all the news media, and they created an atmosphere of tension which held back stock prices in spite of encouraging business news and forecasts.

By 1925, however, the postwar period seemed to have ended. The peace treaties were all signed and ratified. The Washington Conference of 1922 had resulted in a series of agreements in which most major nations accepted partial disarmament. Although France and Belgium occupied the Ruhr when Germany did not pay her reparations on time in 1923, the Dawes Plan of 1924 seemed to set the payments schedule on a realistic basis, with the significant slogan, "business, not politics." America loaned Germany sufficient funds to make the first payments and, from then on, served as a major financial bulwark for that nation. In 1925 Germany and other European nations signed the Locarno pacts, which signified acceptance of the western boundaries drawn after the war. The following year Germany entered the League of Nations. Throughout this period, the Soviets proved incapable of exporting their revolution to the rest of Europe. Insofar as the international scene was concerned, Europe was about to enter a new stage of its history. With this, America felt able to return to the imagined prewar isolationism, and to concentrate its attention on the domestic scene.

4

Investors, Speculators, Bankers, and Rogues

WALL STREET has always been a complex community, but since its earliest days two major groups have both coexisted and contended with each other for leadership. The Establishment, as it came to be called, consisted of leading investment bankers,[1] their allies among smaller houses, and the large companies and important individuals they represented. These men were opposed by the Outsiders, usually lone operators, at times united in temporary alliances, who were often disreputable, tending to violate polite rules when necessary to protect or expand their interests, and who acted as a disruptive influence in contrast to the Establishment's stabilizing effects. In the early nineteenth century Prime, Ward, & King led the Establishment, while Jacob Little was the most famous Outsider. At mid-century, Jay Cooke stood for the Establishment; such colorful characters as Jim Fisk and Daniel Drew made reputations outside the inner circle. Later on J. P. Morgan became the symbol of the Wall Street community, while Bet-A-Million Gates and Thomas Lawson—and to a degree Bernard Baruch—were Outsiders. This distinction continued in the twenties.

At no time in Wall Street history has the Establishment been overthrown, except when members were replaced by others

---

1. The primary function of *investment bankers* is to serve companies and institutions rather than the general public. Thus Morgan & Co. was the investment banker for U. S. Steel, and as such marketed that company's stocks and bonds and in other ways aided in solving financial problems.

who shared its ethic and point of view. The greatest threat to
the Establishment position, however, came during the twenties.
Never before or since have so many new men appeared to gain
power, influence, and leadership. At no time did they attempt
to overthrow the established houses and banks; they could
not have done so in any event. But the new Outsiders were
able to capture the public imagination, exert leadership, and
change the Wall Street Point of View while assuming direction
of the great bull market. Many of the new men had been on
Wall Street before the war, but others appeared in the early
years of the decade. By 1924–1925 they had consolidated their
position; by 1928–1929, they had become folk heroes of a sort.

J. P. Morgan & Co. was still the bulwark of the Establishment in the twenties, although Thomas Lamont and J. P. (Jack)
Morgan Jr. lacked the prestige and power of the founder. Kuhn,
Loeb & Co. retained its perennial number two position, but
Otto Kahn, Mortimer Schiff, and Paul Warburg could not
make or break railroads as had Jacob Schiff a generation earlier.
Dillon, Read & Co. was a major factor in petroleum issues and
foreign securities, while the Rockefellers continued to operate
through the National City Company. Here, too, dynamic, force-
ful leadership was often missing. James Stillman, George F.
Baker, and George Perkins had been giants in the investment
banking community; their successors were often faceless albeit
competent managers. The old firms still did much of the underwriting for large corporations, and exerted tremendous pressures
on the economy, but they no longer held positions of absolute
power.

The reasons for this transformation were not personal, but
rather institutional. The Establishment leaders of the twenties
were well trained, efficient, intelligent, and, when called upon,
daring as well. But conditions had changed to such an extent
that their leadership was no longer necessary. Their predeces-
sors lived at a time when large corporations badly needed reorganization and when ruinous competition made combinations
vitally important to businessmen. From the late nineties through

the first decade of the twentieth century the investment banker's role was to rationalize business and perform the necessary transition from industrial to financial capitalism. By the time of J. P. Morgan's death, this task had been largely accomplished; in the twenties the reorganized corporation was on the way to becoming an autonomous, self-financing entity. In more specific terms, the great age of trust building was over. From 1898–1903 the bankers had acted as mid-wives at the birth of such firms as American Car & Foundry, Union Carbide, U. S. Steel, United Fruit, National Carbon, Diamond Match, Du Pont, Eastman Kodak, U. S. Gypsum, American Tobacco, Corn Products, and many other giants. While combinations continued in the twenties—especially in the steel industry and foods—they were not of the magnitude of the earlier era. Increasingly, investment bankers became servicing rather than initiating forces in the economy. They would float securities for already established companies instead of creating new ones which would dominate their fields.

Another reason for this apparent lack of vitality was that by the early twenties, investment banking had reached a stage similar to that industrial firms achieved in the late nineties. Competition was never as important on Wall Street as elsewhere, but whatever existed was considered wasteful and unnecessary. Firms which had already worked closely together now moved into even greater degrees of collaboration; rarely did a single house attempt to bring out a major issue by itself. Instead, the device of the syndicate was utilized with increasing regularity.

There were three basic types of syndicates in the twenties. The unlimited liability variety was one in which each member agreed to take a specified value of securities and received a proportionate amount of the profits. Whatever securities went unsold were also taken up proportionately, so that while members shared profits, they also spread risks to protect themselves should the underwriting fail. For this reason many smaller houses preferred limited liability syndicates in the early years of the decade. In such an arrangement each member agreed to take a specified value of securities, and was not responsible for the rest should the underwriting fail. Finally, there was the "selling group," in which member firms concerned themselves with retailing securities while a central house, usually a prominent firm, directed wholesale operations.

All of these forms had been utilized earlier in the century, with the limited liability syndicate the most common. Prior to World War I, each house attempted to be as conservative as conditions would enable it to be, and was content to leave risk-taking to the few leaders of the district. Indeed, it was for this very reason that Morgan, National City, and Kuhn, Loeb were able to maintain their pre-eminent positions.

By the mid-twenties, however, the demand for securities had reached a point where even the small houses realized that little risk existed in entering other arrangements. As a result, the unlimited syndicate form gained in popularity, but even more so did the selling group, in which each member vied with the others to sell as many shares as possible so as to maximize profits and commissions.

The demand for new securities was such that most traded at a premium shortly after being publicly offered. Naturally, many rushed to buy in order to "get in on the ground floor" of such "sure things." Like most other houses, the Establishment banks were tempted to use their control over new issues to their advantage and, like the rest, they quickly succumbed to this temptation. Prominent political leaders—the same individuals who were charged with the passage of legislation affecting the economy—were placed on "preferred lists" by leading underwriters. There was nothing underhanded about this; the purchasers were told the issues would be offered to the public at a set price, and that they would have to pay the same price for their securities. In practice, choice issues were often sold out completely to insiders before the public had a chance to take them. The resulting thin market would magnify price movements—usually upward—and so insure windfalls for the lucky few.

By 1927 a new wrinkle had been added: a two-price system. Insiders were able to purchase stocks at one price, while the general public had to pay another, higher price, for the same stock. For example, an offering of Johns-Manville in 1927 sold for $79 a share, but insiders were able to obtain more than 343,000 shares at $47.50 and 56,550 at $57.50, a price differential which came to more than $13 million. In 1929 a Standard Brands flotation was made, and again the insiders shared in the pre-offering distribution. Among their number were former President Coolidge (3,000 shares), Bernard Baruch (4,000 shares), New York Republican National Committeeman Charles Hilles (2,000 shares), former Ambassador and Morgan intimate Norman Davis (500 shares), William G. McAdoo (1,000 shares), General Motors executive and Democratic National Chairman John J. Raskob (500 shares), and future Secretary of the Treasury William Woodin (1,000 shares).

Most preferred lists included Democrats as well as Republicans, since Wall Street hoped for favors from both parties. Although legislators and top members of the executive branch were on several lists, those who operated behind the scenes received the most care from the underwriters. John Raskob, a power in politics and business, was particularly well situated, and was the object of much attention from Wall Street. For example, he was offered the right to purchase 2,000 shares of Alleghany Corporation prior to its official opening at $20 a share. Within a week of the public flotation, the Morgan-sponsored stock was at $33; five months later it reached $57. Naturally Raskob was grateful, as he wrote to Morgan partner George Whitney: [2]

Dear George:

Many thanks for your trouble and for so kindly remembering me. My check for $40,000 is enclosed herewith in payment for the Alleghany stock, which kindly have issued when ready in the

2. United States. 74th Congress, 1st Session, Senate Committee on Banking and Currency, *Stock Exchange Practices* (Washington, 1933), pp. 173–174.

name of John J. Raskob, Wilmington, Delaware. I appreciate deeply the courtesies shown me by you and your partners, and sincerely hope the future holds opportunities for me to reciprocate. The weather is fine and I am thoroughly enjoying golf and sunshine.
Best regards and good luck.   JOHN

In the past, the Establishment houses acted to curb excesses, prevent devious characters from entering the markets, and maintain a spirit of honesty on Wall Street. By the late twenties they had entered into the types of transactions condemned by the elder Morgan and Jacob Schiff and were in no position to call a halt to shady dealings by others. J. P. Morgan had once refused to participate in a Baruch venture because the younger man had used the word "gamble" in describing the operation. "I never gamble," said Morgan, as he terminated the meeting. Now his house and others allied to it were deeply committed to gambles, risky ventures, and other practices which in the past had been left to the Wall Street Outsiders.

The changes in orientation in the board rooms of the old, established investment banks were reflected in and compounded by a new breed of brokers recruited during the decade. In the past, such positions were considered prizes, awarded for faithful and excellent service to those who worked their way up, or to members of the family or friends. With the great expansion in sales, sparked by the stock mania which swept the nation, hundreds of new positions opened in a short time. Branch offices, new firms, and the growth of research facilities caused the supply of positions to outstrip the supply of talent. Necessarily, many posts were filled by individuals who in the past could not have hoped for them, and the glamour of Wall Street and expectations of quick profits attracted brokers whose talents were more suited to the race track or bucket shops.[3] Others turned to Wall Street as the road to an easy sustenance. One

3. A *bucket shop* is an illegal brokerage run by disreputable non-Exchange members. The term is derived from the London Exchange, and is believed to have originated from paupers who carried a bucket from tavern to tavern, gathering the dregs from beer glasses.

of these, Matthew Josephson, returned to America from Paris surrealist circles in 1924. He had a Columbia education, an interest in poetry, art, philosophy, and history, and no training at all in finance.

A newspaperman of my acquaintance who had "covered" the financial district for many years sent me with his warm regards recommendations to a friend who was a member of the Stock Exchange; and so I was engaged. I had to borrow money in order to make my appearance in Wall Street in a new, well-creased suit of clothes.[4]

Josephson received a two-week cram course on stock market techniques, and was then given a desk; he was ready to advise customers on securities purchases worth many thousands of dollars. Thirty years earlier, a person with his background would never have achieved such a desk, or received more than an interview from a member firm. But in 1928 such untutored individuals sold millions of shares of stock. What is more, many issues they recommended rose; in the bull market which began late in the year every purchase seemed to work out well. From time to time there were "corrections," but then the rise would continue. Wall Street had been inundated with thousands of new men, few of whom had any idea of what a bear market or panic could do. The last of the major panics had been in 1907, at a time when many young customers' men [5] were still in grade school. In effect, uninitiated brokers were selling stocks to an uninformed public. And stocks were being *sold* in the mid- and late twenties. The new customers' men were little different from salesmen in other fields, such as autos or household appliances. They had their quotas, received bonuses for high volume, and praise for activity. The internal literature of the period re-

4. Matthew Josephson. *Life Among the Surrealists* (New York, 1962), p. 278.

5. A *customers' man* is a representative of a securities firm; it is his function to deal with buyers and sellers of stocks and bonds, who are known as his clients. Today most customers' men prefer to be called *registered representatives*.

flected this. In 1929 a large, respected investment house circulated the following memo:

We anticipate a reasonable supply of new issues. Some of them will be easy sellers and some will be difficult, but for us to do our full duty, it is essential that we be prepared to sell any issue of securities which this company buys, regardless of whether it is hard or easy to sell.[6]

If the standards of the Establishment were lower in the twenties than previously, then those of the Outsiders were all but nonexistent. In the past there had been raiders on Wall Street, but only once before, in the post–Civil War era of Daniel Drew, Jay Gould, and Jim Fisk, had they managed to institutionalize themselves in such a way as to constitute a semipermanent threat to the Establishment. Far more common, then, were individuals who tried a single great *coup* and withdrew, or the pool managers who attempted a corner, completed it, and then retired from such activities.

In the early twenties, before the speculative fever began, there were several spectacular corners [7] of the type mentioned, as well as a plethora of petty grifters who had always plagued the securities markets. In late March 1920, the newspapers reported that Earl Victor Broughton von Brandenburg, a freelance writer who operated under the name of Broughton Brandenburg, was convicted of selling stock in a bogus mine. In the same month six bucket shop operators were convicted of fraud. In March, too, Allen A. Ryan, the son of the famed financier Thomas Fortune Ryan, began his corner in Stutz Motors. The firm was sound financially, though small; in 1919 Stutz sold less than $7.3 million worth of cars and showed a profit of $1.6 million. More important, it had only 100,000 shares of common stock outstanding and Ryan, the Chairman of its board, held a large block of these.

    6. George Edwards. *The Evolution of Finance Capitalism* (New York, 1938), pp. 234–35.
    7. A *corner* is said to exist when an individual or group has purchased most of the existing supply of a firm's stock, with the hope of advancing its price and making a profit thereby.

Stutz was never an active issue but on Monday, March 8, it began to trade in large volume as its price rose. By March 12 the bears entered the Stutz situation, selling short in expectation of a fall,[8] at which time they would buy stock needed to cover their sales. But the decline did not develop; instead prices moved upward sharply.

Transactions and Prices of Stutz Motors, March 1920

DAY	VOLUME	OPEN	HIGH	LOW	CLOSE	CHANGE
1	100	113	113	113	113	— 2¾
2	300	113	113¾	113	113¾	+ ¾
3	No Trade					
4	700	114¾	118	114¾	118	+ 4¼
5	100	122	122	122	122	+ 4
6	900	123	125	123	123½	+ 1½
8	2,000	124	129	123½	129	+ 5½
9	2,100	129	131½	126	131½	+ 2½
10	1,800	131	135	131	135	+ 3½
11	1,300	134	137	134	135⅞	+ ⅞
12	3,100	136	142	136	140	+ 4⅛
13	1,500	139	144½	139	143¼	+ 3¼
15	2,800	144½	151	144½	150	+ 6¾
16	2,000	151⅛	153	149	152	+ 2
17	4,200	151⅛	169¾	149¼	169½	+17½
18	4,100	180	190	180	190	+20½
19	4,500	190	204	190	204	+14
20	4,600	206	220	206	220	+16
22	4,300	225	228	216	225	+ 5
23	2,300	232	245	230	245	+20
24	5,000	243	250	237	248	+ 3
25	4,300	245	282	245	282	+34
26	7,400	295	325	295	324	+42
27	600	330	330	318	318	— 6
29	3,200	315	337	300	329	+11

SOURCE: *New York Times,* March 1–30, 1920.

8. A *bear* is one who has a pessimistic view of the market and economy, and expects prices to fall. He is, then, the opposite of a bull. Bears will sell securities, expecting to profit from the fall. *Short selling* is a favorite bear device. It consists of selling shares borrowed from others. When the price has declined, the bear will purchase sufficient shares on the open market to repay his loan. This is called "covering

Trading in Stutz was suspended on March 29. By then Ryan owned or held contracts for 110,000 shares—10,000 more than were outstanding.[9] Within hours Wall Street read of Ryan's actions. "I do not want to hurt the public," he said. "I bought these securities because I believe in them." Nonetheless, the Board of Governors was firm; on June 25 Ryan was expelled from the New York Stock Exchange.

The Stutz corner was important for three reasons, all of which indicate that it marked the end of an era. In the first place, the Board found Ryan guilty of manipulations, acted firmly in suspending trading, and finally expelled the guilty party. Had such swift actions been duplicated in the many other, more spectacular corners of the twenties, perhaps speculation would not have been so intense. Next, the public learned of the corner; full disclosure was made. For the rest of the decade, there would be rumors of corners and syndicates, but few investigations. As a result, many speculators came to believe that a few powerful individuals were able to cause prices to rise and fall almost at will, and that the Exchange would not

---

a short sale." For example, a bear may decide that U. S. Steel, selling for $100 a share, is due for a decline. He may then borrow U. S. Steel shares from a broker (for a fee) and sell them at $100 at the Exchange. Then, should the stock's price decline to $80, he might purchase shares at that price and "cover his short position" by delivering them to the broker he had borrowed them from earlier. In this case, the bear's profit would be $20 a share, less commissions and fees.

9. Ryan began his purchases early in March, causing the price of Stutz common to rise. Believing the price to be inflated, bears began to sell Stutz short around March 11. By the end of the week a pattern had developed: bears would borrow Stutz from brokers to sell at the market to Ryan, who would then lend the newly purchased shares to brokers, who would then lend them to other bears. In this way, Ryan could accumulate more shares than existed; since the transactions were on paper—with the bears never seeing the borrowed shares—Ryan was able to purchase the same shares twice.

Some bears began to panic on March 17, and attempted to cover their short positions by purchasing Stutz at the open market. These purchases caused the price to rise still further, leading to more short covering and still higher prices. The panic reached its height on March 26, when bears bid for Stutz, and found the supply had dried up. At this point, as the *corner was culminated,* Ryan *squeezed the shorts.*

prevent them from so acting. In large measure they were correct. Finally, the corner was carried out by an insider, one who had a position in the firm involved. In most of the major corners of the past, insiders had participated to a greater or lesser degree. When Drew, Gould, and Fisk manipulated the stock of Erie Railroad, they were also officers in the corporation. Although most insiders considered their firms little more than vehicles for speculation, they were businessmen as well as gamblers, and they realized how the economy operated. The major speculators of the twenties were all Wall Street figures; none were engaged in business operations as well. They all knew the Exchange and how it functioned, but few had any inkling of the relationship between the economy and stock prices.

Conditions in the twenties—especially after 1924—were such that bears went bankrupt. In a rising market, even the most dour bear was converted to the bull side. As a result, by 1928 the bullish influence of Outsiders operated to push prices higher than was reasonable. By then, the important Outsiders were convinced of their own omnipotence. This is understandable when we consider that, like the new customers' men, they had never known a panic. With few exceptions, the leading manipulators of the twenties were new men, who had been in other fields prior to the war. Their social and religious backgrounds were strikingly different from those of the Establishment. Few were college graduates—none of those who had been to college had attended the Harvard–Yale–Princeton trinity. While the Establishment was dominated by Episcopalians, Presbyterians, and German Jews, many Outsiders were Catholics or East European Jews. The Establishment was based in the East, within the New York–Boston–Philadelphia triangle. Leading Outsiders came from the Midwest and Far West; Chicago was strongly represented.

Although the Outsiders were frowned upon by the Establishment, they nonetheless complemented each other's actions. The old Wall Street houses provided brokerage services for the general public, but in the main acted to draw the large corporations and important public and private individuals into the market. The Outsiders, who in time became almost fabled figures, intrigued the general public. Should rumors of their activities in a certain stock take hold, that stock would rise sharply on heavy volume, and thousands of small investors would attempt to hop on the bandwagon. Between them, then, the Establishment and the Outsiders managed to draw almost every segment of society into speculation in the twenties.

Wall Street received a portent of things to come in 1923. Clarence Saunders, president of Piggly-Wiggly Stores, had been angered by a bear raid on his company's stock the previous November. Now he planned their destruction; Saunders would execute a corner in Piggly-Wiggly, trapping the bears and ruining them. The bear raid had forced the stock's price down from the 50s to below 40. Saunders brought in Jesse Livermore, whose buying sent Piggly-Wiggly to 75½ by March 20. At this point Livermore called upon the shorts to deliver; when they were not able to because of the corner, the price rose to 124.[10] Late that afternoon Piggly-Wiggly was suspended from trading, but the Governors allowed the bears extra time to deliver their stock. Saunders protested; such action was contrary to Exchange rules. But the Governors would not budge. In the end, Saunders was ruined, but Livermore emerged with an enhanced reputation as a market manipulator.

10. A *bear raid* occurs when a speculator or group decides to sell stock in a firm and so force its price downward. Afterward the group would cover its short positions and so show a profit. In this case, the bears selected Piggly-Wiggly common and established large short positions in the stock, which was then sold on the market, forcing its price to new lows. Saunders retaliated by organizing a bull pool which, led by Livermore, purchased all the shares the bears had to offer—and more. The struggle was resolved when the bears, unable to lower Piggly-Wiggly's price, decided to cover their positions by purchasing shares at prices higher than those at which they had gone short. These covering purchases caused the stock's price to rise still further, and resulted in Exchange action. The Piggly-Wiggly manipulations were the first of many struggles between bull and bear groups in the 1920s.

The key figure in the Piggly-Wiggly episode was Jesse Livermore, who for the rest of the decade would make fortunes manipulating stocks for others and, on occasion, for his own account. Livermore was one of the few Outsiders who had been on Wall Street during the 1907 panic, an event which made him a bear for years. Until the mid-twenties, he took seriously the old Wall Street aphorism that speculators are born bulls and wind up as bears; for the most part, he was on the selling side of the market. But, by then, Livermore had bowed to the trend and turned "bullish." In the interim, he became a careful student of the market, and from time to time tried to make public his philosophy of speculation. "My principal method is to study the effect of present and future conditions on the earning power of the various companies engaged in different lines of industry," he said. "Anticipation of coming events is the whole thing. When I have my mind made up about this, I wait for the psychological moment. I do not deal promiscuously; instead, I decide how much I will trade in, and how much money I will risk on that trade, and then I buy or sell the whole quantity at once." [11] Within days of a Livermore maneuver, word would be leaked to the press and public, and hundreds of his followers would attempt to buy or sell as their leader had done. Thus, Livermore's buys went up when word reached small investors, whose subsequent purchases caused them to rise, while Livermore's short sales were equally successful, since the selling and shorting that followed them would inevitably cause prices to fall. Self-fulfilling prophecy was a key to Livermore's actions; he could always count on his followers to cause his predictions to come true.

Livermore was the most famous of the Outsiders, but there were many others, some bigger dealers than he. Arthur Cutten, a Chicago bookkeeper before the war, made millions through speculations on grain futures and then came to New York to try the stock market. By 1928 he was the central figure in

11. Richard Wycoff. *Wall Street Ventures and Adventures through Forty Years* (New York, 1930), p. 254.

several major syndicates, formed to speculate in various stocks. Cutten preferred petroleum issues, but would try anything that promised a quick profit. In time the Cutten syndicates became more famous if not more powerful than the selling groups of the Establishment. By early 1929 many small speculators had come to believe that Cutten could cause a major panic through his selling activities, or maintain the boom indefinitely through his bull pools. Since Cutten, along with most of his group, was usually on the bull side of the market, his activities served to keep prices high, as the "little fellow" bought securities which might interest insiders like him and sold those which were not "movers."

Michael J. Meehan, a former ticket broker, was to the Outsiders what J. P. Morgan & Co. had become for the Establishment: a major banker who hoped to dominate his fellows. M. J. Meehan & Co., headed by "Mike" and his circle—Esmonde O'Brian, Richard O'Brian, John Moyland, and J. P. McKenna—was also a major force behind most of the pools in RCA, the leading glamour stock of the decade. By 1927 Meehan had purchased seven Exchange seats with his profits, had offices throughout the nation and on airships and ocean liners, and was planning still greater bull pools in Radio. Together with the Fisher brothers, whose sale of their company to General Motors had made them multimillionaires, he organized syndicates for other issues as well.

There were dozens of individuals involved in the large pools of the late twenties. But rich and powerful as they were, their activities would have come to little were it not for the huge followings they had among the general public. The Outsiders realized this and assiduously worked at the spreading of rumors, the planting of tips, and the corrupting of individuals charged with responsibility by newspapers and radio stations. A. Newton Plummer, a former publicity man, was hired by several pool managers to place items in newspapers. Plummer soon found that some financial columnists were not above taking sums of money to print his stories. Richard Edmondson of the *Wall*

Street Journal, Charles Murphy of the New York *Evening Mail,* William Gomber of *Financial America,* J. F. Lowther of the New York *Herald Tribune,* W. F. Walmsley of *The New York Times,* and William White of the New York *Evening Post* were among those who received checks from Plummer in this period. Although these men were never indicted, they lost their jobs. It was shown that they had printed stories about stocks which Plummer favored. John J. Levinson, a pool manager for Borg-Warner and Celotex common stock, maintained constant communication with Raleigh Curtis, whose column "The Trader" appeared in the New York *Daily News.* Curtis could be counted upon to speak highly of any stock Levinson chose to buy. William J. McMahon, president of the McMahon Institute of Economic Research and a radio commentator on the stock market, took many of his items from pool manager David Lion. Although all of these connections remained hidden until the early days of the New Deal, it was common knowledge on Wall Street that newspapermen were being paid, newscasters were working in conjunction with speculators, and that formerly trusted news sources were in all probability linked with one syndicate or another. Interestingly, there were no major investigations of these connections. Instead of demanding an end to such chicanery, speculators considered them part of the game; they did not want to end the shady deals, but merely tried to become "insiders" themselves. Tipsters and confidence men, always a scourge of the financial district, were by 1929 almost respectable and an accepted part of the Wall Street scene.

There is no way of knowing how many individuals followed the planted news stories or acted upon advice radio commentators gave. For that matter, students of the period differ in their approximations of the number of people involved in the stock market in the twenties. An Exchange estimate, made in 1929, was that some 20 million Americans owned stocks. But later it was disclosed that this figure contained many duplications, since it was merely a total of reported shareholders by each company; the owner of ten stocks would be counted that many times. Joseph McCoy, chief actuary of the Treasury, thought that some 3 million Americans held securities for investment in 1928, but this figure excludes the in-and-out traders who accounted for a disproportionate amount of the trading volume. Member firms reported a total of slightly more than 1.5 million accounts in 1929, a figure which includes individuals who purchased one share and those who dealt in thousands, and does not allow for individuals with more than one account. It is possible to obtain figures for call loans, but there are none for the number of people who purchased stocks on margin. Estimates for this group run from 500,000 to 750,000. Insofar as market activity was concerned, this last category was the most important. Investors provided a solid base for the market but the traders, especially those with margin accounts, were the ones who caused prices to rise and fall.

If we cannot measure the number of such speculators accurately, or demonstrate that it was their activity which gave the market of the late twenties its particular character, we can see evidence of their impact. The key figure here is the amount of brokers' loans. At the beginning of the decade, there were approximately $1 billion in such loans outstanding. By early 1926, when it seemed certain that the bull market was going to continue, they had risen to $2.5 billion. Two years later the figure was $3.5 billion. During the spectacular trading days of 1928 demand rose sharply, and by January 1, 1929, call loans were well over $6 billion. By early October 1929 more than $8.5 billion in loans were outstanding. Since there is reason to believe the number of margin accounts did not increase proportionately from 1927 to October 1929, it appears that speculators were making greater use of the call money market than they had earlier; instead of owning tens of thousands of dollars worth of securities on small margins, they held hundreds of thousands on still smaller amounts of margin, borrowing more heavily than ever before.

Prices on the Exchange seem to have reflected this. Naturally, most issues moved upward in the bull market, but stock splits and stock dividends were calculated in such a way as to keep the prices of rapidly moving issues around the $100 mark—the most popular for some reason with the margin buyers. One hundred shares of a $100 stock could be purchased with as little as $1,000 in 1929.[12]

These high prices also seemed to magnify the bull market. To the unsophisticated, a 10-point advance on a $100 stock appeared more dramatic than a one-point move for a $10 stock, although in terms of percentage they were identical. Individuals who before the war had earned $25 a week and were now in the $75 category—members of the broad middle class—drove Chevrolets purchased on time, wore clothes bought on credit, and had radios, cigarette lighters, appliances, and medical care on "easy payment plans." Should they die, their funerals could be provided with so much down and so much per month. By the mid-twenties they were buying stocks on margin. Somehow the ownership of securities, even when on 10 per cent margin, lifted them from the middle class to the upper reaches. A share of Gulf Oil made you the partner of Secretary Mellon; a share of General Motors united you with John J. Raskob. In 1926 one could purchase 100 shares of RCA at 32; using margin, the cost could be as little as $320 plus commission. For this amount of money, the $75-a-week salesman could ride Mike Meehan's coattails, become a silent partner in the bull syndicates, and participate in the rapidly growing radio and electrical industries. By 1928 the shares could be sold for $42,000; the speculator's profits, after paying his loan, would exceed $38,000. Participation in the bull market gave one a feeling of power, excitement, and enjoyment, as well as providing

12. In contrast, the most popular price for active issues in the sixties is from $20 to $40. Since most purchasers today pay cash for their stock, it means that a $20 issue would require $2,000 plus commission. In effect, then, today's buyer of what in 1929 would be considered a low-price issue actually puts up more money in terms of cash than 1929's purchaser of $100 stocks.

a ladder to the upper class. No wonder the markets attracted the uninitiated; it is not surprising that speculators and rogues of 1920 had become the farsighted believers in the American dream to thousands of small investors by 1928, and that investment bankers and market raiders became folk heroes before the crash.

5

The Exterior Threat: Insull, Kreuger, and the Van Sweringens

ONE OF THE most fundamental economic laws is that of supply and demand, and nowhere was it more apparent than on Wall Street. When the demand for a security exceeded its supply, the price rose; should there be a greater supply than demand, its price would fall. Throughout the history of Wall Street speculators and manipulators attempted to circumvent this simple fact, but they were never able to ignore it for long. By the mid-twenties there was a great demand for securities in America, one which far outstripped the supply. New issues were grabbed by eager speculators even before they were announced; most sold at a premium minutes after being subscribed for by insiders and those lucky few who were able to buy at the offering price. No wonder, then, that investment bankers competed with one another for the favors of businessmen who might want to float a new stock issue or borrow through bond flotations. Money was cheap; stocks and bonds were dear. It was a golden age for those who had the intelligence, imagination, and daring to take advantage of the situation—to make full use of the law of supply and demand.

Samuel Insull,[1] who later became the Chicago utilities ty-

1. Samuel Insull was one of the most glamorous figures of his time, though personally he was a quiet, rather shy individual. Born in England, he came to America in 1881 to become Thomas A. Edison's secretary. Insull's talents were quickly recognized by the disorderly Edison, and the

coon, had difficulty financing his operations shortly after the war. "Bankers will lend you umbrellas only when it doesn't look like rain," was his wry comment in 1919. But by mid-decade, the situation had changed:

Assuming command during the expansionist fever of the late twenties, they began throwing money at everyone who seemed prosperous; Insull they deluged with easy credit, begging him to accept it, for any purpose. At a party, the new president of the Continental Bank sidled up to Junior and, with the manner of a French postcard peddler, said, "Say, I just want you to know that if you fellows ever want to borrow more than the legal limit, all you have to do is organize a new corporation, and we'll be happy to lend you another $21,000,000." As Philip McEnroe, Insull's bookkeeper, said, "The bankers would call us up the way the grocer used to call my mamma, and try to push their money at us. 'We have some nice lettuce today, Mrs. McEnroe; we have some fresh green money today, Mr. Insull. Isn't there something you could use maybe $10,000,000 for?' " [2]

Such openhandedness was welcomed by the Insull forces, who used bankers to great advantage in the next few years. It was also in striking contrast to what had gone earlier; for the previous two decades, Insull had faced tight money insofar as his projects were concerned.

More than any other field of industrial enterprise, electric power generation and distribution required heavy capital investment. It was considered impossible to survive in the industry without close connections with the investment banking community, which would float securities, refinance debts, and in other ways provide financial services for the utility. Insull had poor relations with the Morgan interests, and so was effectively kept out of New York's financial markets. In order to survive

young Englishman soon moved into more responsible positions. By 1884 he was Edison's unofficial business manager, and, as such, battled Morgan when Edison thought the banker was taking too great an interest in the Edison Electric Light Company. Eight years later Insull left Edison to become head of the Chicago Edison Company. In 1912 he founded Middle West Utilities, a holding company which managed and acquired operating firms in the Midwest.

2. Forrest McDonald. *Insull* (Chicago, 1962), p. 278.

and grow, he had to develop new forms and methods of raising capital. One was consumer ownership; each of the operating companies in Middle West Utilities had a department devoted to securities distribution, which was consolidated at the top in Utilities Securities Company. The U.S.C. concentrated on selling stocks to users of Middle West Utilities power, and did so with striking success in the early twenties.

Debt flotation presented another, more difficult problem. In order to gain the millions of dollars needed for new plant and equipment, Insull joined forces with Harold L. Stuart of Halsey, Stuart & Company. Like Insull, Stuart was not a member of the Wall Street inner circle. A devoted Chicagoan, he saw no reason why businesses in his city had to travel to Wall Street to gain financing. In an age when Chicago aspired to become the leading city in the nation, Stuart attempted to join with Insull to provide a combination to rival Morgan.

As the decade wore on, the Insull complex added more and more companies, which required additional capital expenditures and greater flotations by Halsey, Stuart. As already indicated, the money came in with little difficulty; the Insull firms were efficient, well managed, and technologically advanced. On the other hand, all was not as well as it appeared. Insull firms under the Middle West Utilities umbrella showed excellent profits and growth rates in excess of similar firms in other parts of the country. This made them better credit risks, facilitated securities flotations, and encouraged many small companies to join the holding company. Later on it was learned that the profit statements were padded through securities transactions entered into by the firms. Middle West Utilities would order one operating unit to purchase securities from another at a price which would show a large profit for the second company, a sum then included in the year-end profit statements. In return, the second company would purchase securities from the first, which would then have its own large profit to declare. In January of 1928, Middle West Utilities sold securities to a controlled firm, National Electric Power, for a $3 million profit.

Under the same agreement, National Electric sold other securities to Middle West, also for a profit of approximately $3 million. Thus, the two firms were able to claim substantial capital gains, which inflated earnings, and in turn led to higher prices for the securities and greater ease in debt flotation. This maneuver was completely legal, but also misleading, to say the least.

In 1927 the House of Morgan announced the formation of the United Corporation, a multi-billion-dollar utility holding company which, according to insiders, would become the U. S. Steel of the industry. The New York bankers made it quite clear that they would soon invade Insull territory. Soon after, Cyrus S. Eaton of the Cleveland banking house of Otis & Company began to purchase stock of Commonwealth Edison, People's Gas, Public Service, and Middle West Utilities. Foiled in an earlier attempt to gain control of some Morgan companies, he was now preparing a giant raid on Insull companies.

Faced with threats from New York and Cleveland, Insull and Stuart acted to shore up their finances. In December of 1928, they formed a new investment company, Insull Utility Investments, which owned large blocks of stock in the operating companies already under the Insull banner. Insull was to hold controlling interest in I.U.I., and through it combat raiders and outsiders. The stock was offered at $12 a share, with the usual list of insiders taken care of in the initial flotation. It opened trading at 25 and closed its first day at 30. Within a half year it was selling at more than 150. In the giant bull market of 1929, I.U.I. and constituent firms were volume leaders, and all seemed to rise without limit. In January, Commonwealth Edison sold at 202; by August it was 450. In the same period Middle West Utilities went from 169 to 529. In late July and August Insull-connected companies appreciated by more than half a billion dollars, at a rate of $7,000 a minute around the clock.

In order to take advantage of the public's insatiable desire for securities, Insull and Stuart organized a new holding company, Corporation Securities of Chicago. Just as in the past

Insull firms bought and sold securities from each other, so I.U.I. and "Corp." were completely inter-connected. I.U.I. owned 28.8 per cent of Corp., while Corp. held 19.7 per cent of I.U.I. Together they controlled four great holding companies: Middle West Utilities (111 subsidiaries); People's Gas, Light & Coke (8 subsidiaries); Commonwealth Edison (6 subsidiaries); Public Service Co. of Northern Illinois (1 subsidiary). In addition, these four holding companies together controlled Midland United Company (30 subsidiaries). The entire complex had assets of over $2.5 billion, and served more than 4.5 million customers. Each group member had its own securities flotations, but all were dominated by the Insull interests. The slightest increase in earnings at the bottom was magnified many times at the top. But weaknesses anywhere in the structure would also be transmitted through interlocking ownership to healthy parts of the system. Similar situations existed at United Corporation and Electric Bond & Share, utility holding companies that were even larger than the Insull complex. The major differences between these two and the I.U.I.–Corp. combination was that their capitalizations were simpler and less responsive to sudden fluctuations, and both were intimately connected with the Wall Street Establishment. This would spell the difference between survival and collapse in the early thirties.

The Insull pattern also appeared in Cleveland, where the Van Sweringen brothers used holding companies with great effectiveness in attempting a widespread railroad consolidation. On the surface at least, the two operations seemed similar. Both were led by non–New Yorkers, both were noted for the pyramiding of one company upon several others, and both were glamorous to investors of the late twenties. But there was one important difference: the Van Sweringens worked in harmony with some of Wall Street's leading figures and, although not part of the Establishment themselves, did not oppose it.

Oris Paxton and Mantis James Van Sweringen were as improbable as their names. Oris was two years older than Mantis, but they seemed so alike that strangers took them for twins. Both were bachelors who had never gone beyond the eighth grade in school. They lived together, worked together, and even slept in twin beds. Both began their careers as office boys and drifted into real estate in the twilight of Cleveland's great expansion in the early part of the century. Together they designed and helped build Shaker Heights, one of the nation's wealthiest and most beautiful communities. By the end of the war, the Van Sweringens had reputations as builders and good businessmen, connections in the New York money market, and $500,000 in cash.

The Van Sweringens also had a marginal interest in railroads. The nation's railroads, especially in the Midwest, were in poor condition. The war had enabled most to show good profits, but many bankers thought hundreds of smaller lines might go bankrupt after the armistice. For a while it seemed that the roads would be nationalized to save them from this fate, but the plan was soon abandoned. The lines needed reorganization; an opportunity was present for anyone who might be interested. Shaker Heights was on the outskirts of Cleveland, tied to the city by antique streetcar lines. In order to make their properties more attractive, the brothers decided to construct a high-speed electric line. In searching for a proper terminal, their plans conflicted with those of the managers of the New York, Chicago & St. Louis Railroad (the "Nickel Plate") who wanted the same location for their own company. After some negotiations, the matter was resolved when the brothers agreed to purchase control of the Nickel Plate from the New York Central. The price was $8.5 million; all the brothers had was their half million and an equal amount raised from friends. The Van Sweringens took the problem to their bankers and received a quick solution: form a holding company (the Nickel Plate Securities Co.), keep enough shares for control, and then sell the rest to the public. The brothers followed this advice and were able to raise more than the $7.5 million needed. Now they were in the railroad business.

The Nickel Plate was reorganized and showed a dramatic

increase in profits. This enabled the Van Sweringens to float more securities and make small fortunes from their investment. Deciding that they had a talent for railroading, they sold off their real estate interests and began a search for other promising properties.

Shortly thereafter the brothers found three small but growing lines. In order to pay for them they sold preferred stock in Nickle Plate Securities, again receiving more money than necessary. A sale of Nickel Plate bonds paid for a 15 per cent interest in the huge Chesapeake & Ohio in 1925. Then came the Pere Marquette, also through borrowing. In 1927 the brothers became interested in the Erie, a large line which had been robbed by generations of adventurers. George F. Baker, the old Morgan confidant, was the largest stockholder in the Erie. He arranged to meet the brothers and was sufficiently impressed to allow them to take over. Naturally, such a move cost many millions, and again the Van Sweringens floated bonds, formed holding companies, and sold stock: the money was raised.

By the end of the decade the flotations, amalgamations, and manipulations had resulted in a chaotic jumble of companies which, taken together, made the brothers one of the most important forces in transportation. At the top of the Van Sweringen pyramid were the General Securities Corporation and the Vaness Co. The brothers owned 40 per cent of G.S.C. and 80 per cent of Vaness. Since Vaness owned an additional 50 per cent of General Securities, control of both was assured.

General Securities controlled Alleghany Corporation, which controlled Chesapeake Corporation, which controlled the Chesapeake & Ohio Railroad. The C. & O. in turn held stock in other lines, together with Vaness, General Securities, Alleghany, and the Chesapeake Corporation. The Wheeling & Lake Erie, the Kansas City Southern, the Chicago & Eastern Illinois, the Missouri Pacific, and the Denver & Rio Grande were also in the Van Sweringen web. So complex was the pyramid that the brothers' equity in the small Hocking Valley was only .25 per cent, but they controlled it nonetheless. Much of this was be-

yond Oris' and Mantis' comprehension; their lawyers and ac-
countants took care of such details. The brothers' simplicity
came out in testimony in 1933. Ferdinand Pecora, counsel
during the Congressional investigations following the 1929 crash,
asked Oris a question regarding the organization of his interests.
Oris was unable to answer directly, and had to speak to his
advisors before making his statement.

MR. VAN SWERINGEN (*after conferring with his associates*): The
statement I made about that, which I again make, was this. Chesapeake Corporation and its acquisition of securities was in fact
a re-organization resulting in a mere change in the form of
ownership of property. In its formation General Securities Corporation was organized as a medium for exchanging the Vaness Co.
holdings of Chesapeake & Ohio stock for its stock so as to avail
of the income-tax exemptions provided by Congress in connection
with corporate gains in this circumstance. Just as in the formation of Alleghany, Geneva Corporation was organized as an intermediate step in the exchanges involved in that instance.
MR. PECORA: Now, that answer is read from a prepared statement,
is it not?
MR. VAN SWERINGEN: It is.
MR. PECORA: And did you prepare it?
MR. VAN SWERINGEN: I did. After some little difficulty to get the
details of the transaction. Perhaps I should say the intricacies of
the transaction.[3]

These complexities and mysteries only served to enhance
the reputation of the Van Sweringens in the late twenties. Like
Insull, they were considered workers of marvels, the logical
next step in the development of American capitalism. More
important insofar as the investment community was concerned,
stocks in the Van Sweringen empire rose steadily, enabling investors to reap profits while the brothers floated new issues of
stocks and bonds, which were well received both by insiders and
the general investing public.

The Van Sweringen pyramid was complex. At cocktail

3. United States, Senate, Committee on Banking and Currency,
*Subcommittee on Banking and Currency, Stock Exchange Hearings
Practices* (Washington, 1932–34), pp. 717–18.

parties customers' men and investment bankers would try to explain how it worked, usually with little success. On the other hand, it did seem explainable; the facts seemed to be public. Such was not the case with Ivar Kreuger, whose activities were shrouded in mystery and who himself was an enigmatic figure.

In the twenties many Americans were fascinated by stories of European mystery figures. Count Basil Zaharoff, for example, was credited with having started several Balkan wars through munitions deals. Spy stories, tales of intrigue, and malfeasance in high places multiplied during the several disarmament conferences of the decade, and remained a favorite with readers of the Sunday supplements afterwards. Stories of world-wide cartels, clandestine deals which netted millions of dollars in a matter of hours, were readily accepted during the bull market. Unfortunately for American investors, however, these manipulations *were* secret; outsiders could not participate. But there was one exception: Ivar Kreuger of Sweden was willing to sell shares in his world-wide holdings to Americans, and Americans were eager to buy them.

Kreuger was known as the Match King; through his various interconnected holdings, this son of a Swedish admiral dominated the world market for matches of all types. Most of his companies were controlled by Kreuger & Toll; his leading subsidiary was International Match. Stocks in both companies were in demand in America. Kreuger floated some $148,500,000 worth of International Match securities in America from 1923 to 1929, and transferred $144,000,000 of this amount to his European holdings; the money was never seen again. Nor would Kreuger allow his American auditors to see his books. Whenever pressed, he would leave the room, return with a handful of documents—many unrelated to the questions asked—and then leave again, always shrouded in an air of mystery.

Ordinarily, such actions would lead to suspicions, fears, and a drop in the price of Kreuger securities. The Kreuger companies paid regular and generous dividends, however, sweetened by extras and increases in payments. When asked why he kept so little of his money in America, Kreuger responded by saying that he did this to avoid American taxes. When an auditor questioned him about the cash balances in one firm and meekly requested a look at the books, Kreuger cabled that "In the matter of Atlas, let me say that a personal examination of the books disclosed a surplus of $150,000 at the moment." But Kreuger would not allow others to see the books. Any fears that such a cavalier attitude might be a sign of financial weakness were dissipated when Kreuger deposited funds for dividend disbursements before the due dates. "We have so much money here," he wrote his New York bankers, "you might as well have this now." On occasion he would send too much money to his bank. When the overpayment was noted, the Match King wrote: "Oh, we simply made a mistake. We have so much money here, we just can't keep track of it." American investors, hearing these stories and other, still more impressive tales of Kreuger power and mastery, rushed to buy more International Match and Kreuger & Toll, sending the prices still higher and enabling the Match King to float additional securities at inflated prices. In all, he took approximately $250 million from American investors until he was unmasked as a swindler in 1932.

Insull, the Van Sweringens, and Kreuger made strange bedfellows. Although they were responsible for the ruin of thousands of investors, the first two left behind legacies of a positive nature, while Kreuger bequeathed nothing to his investors and embarrassment to his bankers and auditors. Insull was quiet and withdrawn, but became a leader of Chicago society and the benefactor of the city's opera. The Van Sweringens, quaint and eccentric, were nonetheless at home with the Wall Street Establishment. Kreuger was later exposed as a sexual pervert as well as a Ponzi of the upper reaches.

Nevertheless, there were points of similarity as well. These men were infused with glamour, the type associated with touches of gold. The investing public gave them the same kind of adulation afforded Henry Ford earlier in the decade and Andrew Carnegie a generation before. Ford and Carnegie were genuine heroes, men who helped organize giant industries which transformed the nation from a small power into the great industrial state it was in the twenties. Insull and the Van Sweringens, though to an extent constructive, were admired because they seemed to have the key to wealth. The fact that this wealth was of a paper variety while Ford's contribution was concrete seemed to make no difference to the speculators of the era. As for Kreuger, his purposeless power was admired *because* of its nature; the fact that a world-wide cartel could exist impressed the public, who did not bother to question what constructive purpose was served by Kreuger & Toll. This question would be asked later on when Insull, the Van Sweringens, and Kreuger were ruined.

These giant heroes of the bull market had still one more thing in common with each other: in their own ways each was a master of *leverage*. Although the term was not common in the early twenties, it was the key to their operations, and a major factor in the bull market. Without leverage, the great gains in the averages would not have been possible, and public participation would have been greatly limited. With it, the market was able to get out of control by 1928, the prelude to disaster the following year.

6

The Magic of Leverage

ONE OF THE oldest and most familiar devices on Wall Street, leverage was well known to most investors and almost all speculators in the mid-twenties. Put simply, it involved the ratio of equity to debt. If a person owned a security outright, he was not using leverage; should he borrow money for a purchase, he was utilizing it. An individual who resorted to brokers' loans or call money in his dealings was conversant with leverage, even if he had never heard the term. So was a non-securities-owning customer who purchased goods on time.

Almost all large American corporations used leverage before, during, and after the twenties. They would borrow money through the issuance of bonds, then invest the money in the company, where hopefully it would be used to earn more than the debt service charges. Without the ability to borrow and a market in which to sell such debt obligations, few corporations could survive in the American capitalist environment. One might say that leverage was a vital aspect of the economy.

Insull, the Van Sweringens, and Kreuger all used leverage to expand their operations, primarily to manipulate the earnings of securities and to control their holdings. Stock analysts noted that borrowed money caused rapid rises in I.U.I., Corp., Alleghany, and Kreuger & Toll, and so made higher prices possible. The reason is easy to illustrate. Consider two corporations, one with a large debt, the other with none at all. Each have 1 million common shares outstanding, no preferred, and show end-of-the-year earnings of $1 million.

CORPORATION "A"		CORPORATION "B"	
Earnings	$1,000,000	Earnings	$1,000,000
Debt Service	500,000	Debt Service	———
Net Earnings	500,000	Net Earnings	1,000,000
Earnings per Share	.50	Earnings per Share	1.00

Let us now suppose that each firm reports earnings of $2 million the following year:

CORPORATION "A"		CORPORATION "B"	
Earnings	$2,000,000	Earnings	$2,000,000
Debt Service	500,000	Debt Service	———
Net Earnings	1,500,000	Net Earnings	2,000,000
Earnings per Share	1.50	Earnings per Share	2.00

Thus, a doubling of earnings results in a 200 per cent increase in Corporation "A" 's net, and a 100 per cent increase for Corporation "B."

The more leverage a firm uses, the greater this effect will be. Everything else being equal, the per share earnings of a leveraged company would rise more rapidly than one without fixed obligations. And as earnings rise, so will the price of the company's securities, which makes it easier to borrow still more money through debt flotation. As a result, by the late twenties, several large companies found themselves in a pleasant spiral: the more they borrowed, the higher their earnings; the higher their earnings, the more they could borrow. This fact was not lost on corporation treasurers. In 1920 the bonded debt of American corporations was some $55.7 billion; by 1925 it stood at $61.2 billion, having reached a peak of $67 billion the year before. Then, as the bull market took off, debt offerings increased in size and frequency. By 1929 almost $77 billion in bonds were outstanding. This meant that leverage was high for American corporations; per share earnings would be magnified in the years of prosperity. But what would happen in a business slump? Would the debt-laden companies be able to meet their swollen fixed costs in a recession? Comptrollers of large corporations did not seem to have considered such a possibility. While it was evident that leverage would magnify earnings and profits on the upswing of a business cycle and bull market, it would cause sharp drops on the downturn. Again, consider our two corporations should earnings fall to $500,000.

CORPORATION "A"		CORPORATION "B"	
Earnings	$500,000	Earnings	$500,000
Debt Service	500,000	Debt Service	———
Net Earnings	———	Net Earnings	500,000
Earnings per Share	0	Earnings per Share	.50

By 1928 the bulls—especially the younger ones—had convinced themselves that such dips could be ignored; as economist Irving Fisher was to proclaim, the economy had reached what seemed to be a permanently high plateau, with great ascents in the making. Accordingly, the more leveraged a situation, the more desirable it would become.

The appeal of leverage, combined with the general sentiment that bulls controlled the market, led to the formulation of plans for great wealth. One of the more interesting of these came from John J. Raskob in 1928. Twenty years earlier, Raskob had been a $3,000-a-year stenographer; now he was a power in the Du Pont complex and a leading bull, having made tens of millions of dollars in the markets. This was Raskob's year. He had helped Al Smith gain the Democratic nomination for the presidency, and would undoubtedly become a major national figure should Smith win the election. A sentimentalist at heart, Raskob entered politics for several reasons, not the least important of which was the anti-Catholic campaign waged against Smith in 1924. A Catholic himself, Raskob left the G.O.P. to take charge of Smith's affairs. His candidate had a reform record, to be sure, but by 1928 Smith was no radical champion of the poor and oppressed. Instead, he wanted to broaden the base of American society; he would not criticize the new capitalism of the twenties, but rather would try to allow more to participate in it.

This was seen in an article written by Raskob for the *Ladies' Home Journal.* Its title was attractive and indicative of the

others in that wild year. By midyear they had left the more limited holding companies, such as I.U.I. and Corp., in the dust.

Even the conservative banking houses organized trusts in the late twenties. One of these—Goldman, Sachs—floated a large issue of Goldman Sachs Trading Corporation on December 4, 1928. Some 900,000 shares were sold at 104, and the underwriters kept an additional 100,000 shares for themselves; Goldman Sachs Trading Corporation began its life with assets of approximately $100 million. Its stock rose quickly, as did its other obligations. Then the Trading Corporation started to buy established trusts. Central States Electric and Shenandoah were taken over through stock transfers; since Shenandoah controlled the Blue Ridge Corporation, that too came under the Goldman Sachs banner. The American Company followed and, by early autumn, optimistic partners at Goldman, Sachs were busy planning other consolidations, to be paid for with additional issues of preferred stocks and bonds, which would make the Trading Corporation still more leveraged.

Even more complex than Goldman Sachs was the United Founders Group, organized by Harris, Forbes. By the end of 1929, the Group had thirteen large investment companies under its umbrella.

The 13 companies of the United Founders Corporation group had numerous other companies loosely affiliated with them largely through stock ownership, and the group was by far the largest group of investment enterprises in the United States. In all, there were affiliated with the United Founders Corporation 22 investment companies including hybrids of investment company and intermediate credit company. Of these, 14 were organized under the exclusive or joint sponsorship of the United Founders Corporation group as constituted at the time. These investment companies in turn at one time or another effectively dominated seven securities distributing enterprises and at least 16 other companies, the largest of which, United States Electric Power Corporation, held joint control of the billion dollar Standard Gas and Electric Company utility empire. The resources so dominated by the United Founders Corporation group were at one time in excess of $2,100,000,000.[1]

At the height of the bull market in 1929, investment trusts had assets (securities holdings) of approximately $4.5 billion. In order to understand their impact on the market, this figure should be contrasted with the $183.5 billion capitalization of all American corporations in 1928. The influence of organized investment trusts was such that they could cause the market to rise or fall at will—or so ran the popular belief of the day. Their power did indeed seem unlimited in 1929. In August of that year, Goldman Sachs alone floated more than a quarter of a billion dollars worth of securities in conjunction with its take-overs. U. S. & Foreign common, which had a negative value at the time of its flotation, sold for $72 a share; its underwriter made between $30 million and $40 million on an investment of $5 million. Owners of U. S. & Foreign had little reason to complain of this. Their marginally owned-leveraged stock was reaching new highs regularly.

The sudden flood of new investment companies together with the large flotations they produced in 1928 and 1929 created two major, inter-related problems. In the first place, the highly leveraged companies were hard pressed to find investments that would appreciate rapidly so as to make good reading for potential speculators and investors. High-flying stocks were naturally in demand but, since these paid small dividends, the return on investment would not be sufficient to leave a large surplus after the bonds and preferred stocks were serviced. In addition, competition for key issues was so intense that they were often bid beyond reasonable prices. But there was one investment that seemed surefire, paid a good return, and was safe: call money.

As speculation intensified and more people purchased stock on margin, the demand for brokers' loans rose rapidly, leading to an increase in the call money rate. The high rates attracted

1. Hugh Bullock. *The Story of Investment Companies* (New York, 1959), p. 36.

money from the investment trusts, which by 1929 were a major factor in that market. At its peak in 1929, Electric Bond & Share had $157,579,000 invested in call loans, and Tri-Continental $62,150,000. American Founders put $23,629,000 in the call market, and most other trusts had large, though lesser, amounts so invested. This money was loaned to speculators, who often used it to purchase shares in the same investment trust that had loaned the money originally! This created a strange situation, which went unnoticed by market analysts of the time. Stock purchases in American Founders were made with money loaned by American Founders itself. As demand increased, the price of the stock went up, as did the call money rate. This meant the company could show higher earnings, which in turn led to still greater demand for the stock, higher rates, and so on. It resembled nothing more than a dog chasing his own tail. Paper values rose without substance, and few thought to question the boom in which all made money and there were few losers.

7

The Making of the Giant Bull

STOCK MARKET crashes are often spectacular and always exciting. Prices tumble, panic is in the air, and the mass of ticker watchers are shrouded in gloom. Often, but not always, banks and corporations issue cheery notices but then close their doors. Many but not all panics are followed by depressions or recessions.

Market crashes are usually visible only in retrospect. If prices tumble but then recover, and go on to new highs, the dip is termed a "correction"; only when they continue to fall does it become a crash. Similarly, the switch from a bull to bear market can best be studied *ex post facto*. Even today, when securities analysts have defined their terms and perfected their techniques far beyond what existed in the twenties, they will offer differing opinions on what the future will bring at any given moment they are asked the question. The Dow theory,[1] considered a basic tool by the majority of analysts, and whose "signals" are taken more seriously than most, is often misleading —which is why the theorists have coined the phrase "false signal." In fact, over the past forty years, signals given under the Dow theory have been wrong about half the time.

1. The *Dow theory* is one of the oldest and most popular theories of stock market behavior. It was first developed by Charles Dow, founder of the *Wall Street Journal,* around 1900. According to Dow (and his disciple William Hamilton), the stock market itself will give signals when a bull or bear market has begun or has ended. The wise speculator —one who can read these signals—may take advantage of them to maximize his profits.

Still, with all these difficulties, it is evident that in 1929 there was a market crash of major proportions—a crash to compare with those of 1893 and 1907. And later there was a panic, one worse than those of 1873 and 1837. All agree that the crash was severe and the panic deep because it followed one of the greatest bull markets in American history. But there is one question which remains unanswered: when did the bull market begin?

Unlike crashes, the origins of bull markets cannot be discerned in retrospect. They begin slowly, gain speed and volume irregularly, and then reach a crest at the end. Picking the first moves, however, is impossible. It might be analogous to ask where the Mississippi River begins—we know it ends in the Gulf of Mexico; or to try to find the moment a person first had a cancerous growth which led to death. Here only theories can be discussed; we have no clear-cut empirical evidence.

Some students of Wall Street claim that the great bull market of the twenties began in 1914. At the time the nation was in a recession, with the market drifting lower. Then came the war. Like every other exchange in the world, the New York market closed, fearful that international liquidity would be destroyed should trading commence. Irving Fisher of Harvard and other leading economists thought the European war would cause the belligerents to sell their American securities to gain funds for munitions; that Europeans would no longer be able to finance American companies; that blockades would cut America from her markets and so destroy the economy. None of this happened. Instead, European gold came to America for safekeeping; Europeans purchased American securities as the safest investment to be had; and the blockade was broken by the British, enabling American firms to make huge profits by selling to the Allies. As a result, when the market opened for limited trading on December 12, 1914, prices on the whole demonstrated slight improvements over the last quotations in July. Then, as corporate profits showed substantial advances at the end of the year, stock prices took off.

Prices of Selected Issues, 1915

STOCK	JAN. 1 CLOSING	DEC. 31 CLOSING
American Smelting & Refining	56¼	108⅛
Baldwin Locomotive	40½	117⅞
Bethlehem Steel	48⅛	459½
General Chemical	165¼	328½
General Electric	139	174
General Motors	81½	500
United States Steel	49⅜	88⅞

SOURCE: *New York Times,* January 2, 1915, January 1, 1916.

Although prices continued to rise during the neutrality period, they fell once America entered the war and restrictions were placed on the economy. As we have seen, the 1919–1920 advance was followed by a sharp decline in 1920–1921, which preceded the next upturn on Wall Street.

The market was uneasy in 1920. Foreign exchange rates fluctuated wildly, causing similar movements in the call money rate. Corners in General Motors and Stutz, evidence of chicanery in the brokerage community, the after-math of the Ponzi affair, fear of radicalism, and finally the explosion of a bomb in front of the House of Morgan in September, all contributed to this feeling of uneasiness. There was a market crash in November which lasted almost a month, and a giant bear raid on December 8. In all, 1920 was a gloomy year for speculators and investors.

Toward the end of the year, however, there were signs that an upturn might be in the making. As the bear pools organized, the bulls were also at work. One of these was Charles Schwab, a founder of Bethlehem Steel, a leading glamour company of the war period. A deadly serious and conservative businessman who rarely took vacations and lavished all his attention on Bethlehem, Schwab was concerned with the market's decline and wanted to do something about it. On December 14 he called a press conference at the Ritz-Carlton to talk about securities prices. "What is the matter with this market?" he asked. "Here is Pneumatic Tool at 60 paying its regular dividend and earning a great deal more. It has a $10,000,000 plant at cash values that is selling for nothing. In fact, Pneumatic Tool is selling for less than its treasury."

Bethlehem Steel is near 50 and its real book value is near 300. It will earn $40 a share this year before charge-offs and between $25 and $30 according to what we can charge off. I charge off every possible thing. I have charged off since the war $100,000,000. We have some little difference with the government on these charge-offs but not much.[2]

By the most conservative bookkeeping methods, then, Bethlehem was selling for around two times earnings.[3] At the same time, the largest industrial enterprise in America, U. S. Steel, was selling for less than six times earnings. Big Steel closed the year at slightly above $80 a share. It earned $16.62 in 1920, and paid a dividend of $5.00. Since according to the rule-of-thumb used at the time, good-grade industrials should sell at approximately ten times earnings, U. S. Steel was underpriced and Bethlehem grossly undervalued by investors.

Prices continued to fall in early January 1921, but brokers issued optimistic statements. "Will business come back?" asked Otis & Brothers. The answer was "Yes." "Our burden is very light compared with the rest of the world." Henry L. Doherty & Company was even more positive. "Perhaps never again will there be such bargains in investment securities as the market now offers and so we say to you all—scrape together all the money you can get without borrowing and buy investment securities—and buy them now."

But the decline continued, though less spectacularly than before. Federal Reserve activities helped stabilize the situation, as did American Telephone & Telegraph's action in raising its dividend from $8.00 to $9.00 in March. In April the Bank of

2. Clarence Barron. *They Told Barron* (New York, 1930), pp. 41–42.

3. The *price/earnings ratio* is a familiar method of determining whether or not the market price of a security is too high or too low. It is calculated by dividing a firm's earnings per share of common stock into its market price. Thus, a stock selling at $100 a share, with earnings of $5.00 a share, is said to be selling at twenty times earnings.

England lowered its rediscount rate, another bullish sign. The decline slowed even more. A bottom was reached in August, after which the rise commenced. From November 1919 to August 1921 the Dow-Jones Industrials had fallen from 119.62 to 63.90.

Prices rose during the second half of 1921, ending the year with gains despite continued poor economic news. U. S. Steel reported earnings of only $2.24, but maintained its dividend. Its stock traded for as much as 86½ at one point, or almost forty times earnings. This alone would indicate that a turn in investor psychology had taken place.

Selected Common Stocks, 1921 [4]

VOLUME	STOCK	DIVIDEND	HIGH AND DATE	LOW AND DATE	CLOSE
632,900	American Can	$ 0	35½ Dec. 15	23½ June 21	34¾
860,054	American Telephone	9.00	119½ Nov. 21	95¾ Jan. 3	114⅞
788	Eastman Kodak	0	690 Feb. 5	596 Nov. 3	635
657,477	General Electric	12.00	143¾ Dec. 3	109½ July 22	139¼
3,521,025	General Motors	1.00	16¼ Jan. 11	9⅝ July 24	10
380,800	Goodrich	0	44⅛ Jan. 11	26⅝ June 24	36⅛
534,670	International Nickel	0	17 May 5	11½ Aug. 24	12
48,510	New York Air Brake	0	89 Feb. 19	47½ Aug. 17	59
271,361	Standard Oil (N.J.)	5.00	192¼ Dec. 15	124½ June 13	182½
587,950	Union Pacific	10.00	131⅞ Nov. 29	111 June 21	126⅛
5,310,610	United States Steel	5.00	86½ May 6	70¼ June 23	84¼

SOURCE: *New York Times,* December 31, 1920.

4. In this and subsequent tables, no account is made for *stock splits* and *stock dividends.* Stock splits refer to the division of a company's common stock. In a three-for-one split, the owner of 100 shares of a stock which sold for $150 a share would receive 300 shares, while the stock's price would be approximately $50 a share. Such splits are desirable, since they increase the marketability of the stock (for some reason, customers seem to prefer low-priced stocks to high-priced issues). Splits are often accompanied by dividend increases and favorable publicity, so the price of the new shares is usually somewhat higher than the equivalent in the old shares. That is why, in the case above, the split shares would probably trade for slightly higher than $50 a share.

Stock dividends refer to the issuance of stock to shareholders, sometimes *in lieu of* cash, but often as a "bonus." Should ABC Co. declare a 3 per cent stock dividend, then the holder of 100 shares would receive three additional shares of the firm's stock.

Nineteen twenty-one was a busy year on Wall Street. The volume figures were not high when compared with those of the present, but in terms of turnover they become much more impressive. Eastman Kodak's total of 788 shares seems ridiculously low today, but in 1920 the firm had only 195,862 shares outstanding, most of these closely held by insiders. Similarly, in the sixties American Can has traded more shares in a week than it did all year in 1920. In the latter year, however, there were only 412,333 American Can common shares outstanding. Similar comparisons could be made for other stocks of the period.

Capitalization of Selected Issues, 1920 and 1967

	COMMON SHARES OUTSTANDING	
COMPANY	1920	1967
American Can	412,333	16,435,575
Eastman Kodak	195,862	80,772,718
General Electric	1,384,300	90,598,309
General Motors	20,101,658	285,172,000
Goodrich	600,000	9,182,178
International Harvester	900,000	28,262,014
New York Air Brake	100,000	1,550,741
Standard Oil (N.J.)	983,383	215,444,330
United States Steel	5,083,025	54,138,137

SOURCES: *Poor's Industrial Section,* 1921; *Moody's Handbook,* 1967.

It can be seen, for example, that half the total common shares of General Electric were traded in 1920, and more than three times the common of Standard Oil of New Jersey. Such activity could lead to exaggerated price movements, and did so in 1921, when recovery was well under way and the financial district was in the midst of a small bull market.

Most stocks hit their lows early in the year, and their highs toward the end, as prices closed on a firm note in 1922. Despite the Piggly-Wiggly corner and other disturbances, the market was decidedly bullish. The upward swing continued into 1923; for the first time since the war, most analysts seemed optimistic about coming events. Activity picked up considerably.

Selected Common Stocks, 1922

VOLUME		DIVIDEND	HIGH AND DATE	LOW AND DATE	CLOSE
3,042,765	American Can	$ 5.00	76½ Nov. 2	32¼ Jan. 6	73¼
806,985	American Telephone	9.00	128¼ Aug. 31	114½ Jan. 4	123
168,965	Eastman Kodak	5.50	90½ Dec. 28	70 July 3	89
238,400	General Electric	8.00	190 Dec. 19	136 Jan. 9	182½
4,510,850	General Motors	.50	15¼ July 7	8⅛ Jan. 31	14¾
37,710	Goodrich	0	44⅞ May 29	28½ Nov. 25	35½
322,650	International Nickel	0	19¾ Apr. 24	11¼ Jan. 9	13⅞
46,300	New York Air Brake	0	41⅝ Sept. 20	24½ Nov. 27	24⅗
1,265,520	Standard Oil (N.J.)	5.00	250½ Oct. 10	169 Mar. 24	194
888,050	Union Pacific	10.00	154¾ Sept. 11	125 Jan. 10	138
8,037,810	United States Steel	5.00	111½ Sept. 16	82 Jan. 6	106⅞

SOURCE: *New York Times,* January 2, 1923.

Early in the year, volume averaged around the half-million mark. Then, as prices leveled off and fell in late summer, volume declined. But the market received support in the autumn, and again trading increased. On November 22, 1,500,000 shares exchanged hands, a postwar high. Although total sales for 1923 were lower than they had been for the previous year, a base was formed in September and October which expanded for the rest of the decade. If we are to measure the bull market in terms of public participation, late 1923 becomes an important benchmark.

Volume on the New York Stock Exchange, 1922–1929

YEAR	VOLUME (SHARES)
1922	260,753,997
1923	237,276,927
1924	282,032,923
1925	452,211,399
1926	449,103,253
1927	576,990,875
1928	920,550,032
1929	1,124,990,980

SOURCE: *New York Times,* 1923–1930.

Selected Common Stocks, 1923

VOLUME	STOCK	DIVIDEND	HIGH AND DATE	LOW AND DATE	CLOSE
6,986,740	American Can	$ 6.00	107⅝ Dec. 17	73½ Jan. 2	104¼
447,300	American Telephone	9.00	128¾ Dec. 14	119⅛ June 29	125⅜
352,150	Eastman Kodak	8.75	115¾ Apr. 3	89¾ Jan. 2	109
390,494	General Electric	8.00	202¼ Dec. 11	167⅝ Sept. 21	196½
3,879,550	General Motors	1.20	17½ Apr. 18	12¾ June 28	15
219,600	Goodrich	2.00	41⅛ Mar. 22	17⅜ Sept. 13	22
636,260	International Nickel	0	16¼ Feb. 16	10⅜ Oct. 26	13¾
165,900	New York Air Brake	4.00	42⅞ Nov. 23	26⅝ Jan. 2	40⅞
2,383,937	Standard Oil (N.J.)	1.00	44¼ Mar. 2	30⅞ July 31	41⅞
682,800	Union Pacific	10.00	144⅞ Feb. 16	124½ Aug. 4	128½
6,731,860	United States Steel	5.00	109⅜ Mar. 21	85½ July 31	94½

SOURCE: *New York Times,* January 1, 1924.

Alexander Dana Noyes was one of those who sensed the transformation. Writing his usual year-end review on January 1, 1924, Noyes said:

It has been a year of steady forward movement in finance and industry. . . . A sharp line of distinction, to be drawn about the end of May, separates an . . . enthusiastic "boom" in American finance and industry—in which high records were made in numerous fields of industrial production—to a 20 or 30 per cent. decline in the later months.

Noyes thought it difficult to predict what might happen in the next twelve months. In January, U. S. Steel reported a record backlog; economic recovery was on the way.

Trading continued strong in early 1924 although prices did not rise rapidly. But somehow the atmosphere of the country was changing. Gradually, almost imperceptibly, the nation seemed to be concerning itself more with questions of the present and future than those of the past. The problems of the World War, reconversion, the Red Menace, Prohibition, and other searing issues of the early twenties receded into the background. Woodrow Wilson died on February 3; on September 3 *What Price Glory,* by Maxwell Anderson and Laurence Stallings opened to excellent reviews. This antiwar play seemed symbolic of the nation's rejection of the Great Crusade and all it implied.

Henry Ford lowered the price of the Model "T" to $290, and on June 10 announced that his firm had produced its 10 millionth auto. Ford had taken seven years to produce the first million; the last million were turned out in 132 working days. On October 15 the German airship ZR-3 completed a transatlantic trip from Friedrichshafen to Lakehurst, New Jersey, where it was taken over by the U. S. Navy and renamed *Los Angeles*. Germany resumed gold payments in 1924. There were record crops in America.

That summer the Democrats nominated John Davis for the presidency toward the end of a bitter convention, and only after 103 ballots had been cast. The Republicans named President Coolidge, who had succeeded in cleaning up the scandals of the Harding era. The Conference for Progressive Political Action formed the Progressive Party and selected Robert La Follette for the presidency. Even then La Follette seemed a relic of a previous age.

All the economic indicators pointed upward in early 1924. And there were further stimulants to the economy. On March 18 the House of Representatives passed the Soldiers' Bonus Bill. After the Senate concurred the bill was vetoed by Coolidge, but repassed over his veto and became law in May. Congress also approved the Revenue Act of 1924, which, as we have seen, was the second of the Mellon tax cuts.

All the preconditions for a boom were in the making early in the year. What was needed, perhaps, was a dramatic event to set off the next rise in securities prices. This came in November. The overwhelming victory of President Coolidge over Davis and La Follette seemed an endorsement of Republican prosperity and an assurance of its permanence. The market had been rising throughout the campaign, in anticipation of the election results. Now prices took off on heavy volume. For some market historians, this event signaled the beginning of the great bull market of the twenties.

As can be seen, most stocks hit their highs for the year in November and December. The bull market continued into 1925.

There was wild speculation on Wall Street in January, with prices up sharply across the board and brokers' loans reaching the $1.8 billion figure; by March there were more than $2 billion in such loans outstanding. Despite a sudden fall in November, prices rallied early in December to close the year with sizable gains.

The Dow-Jones statistics indicate a jump in 1925, greater than those of the preceding three years. In addition, for the

Selected Common Stocks, 1924

VOLUME	STOCK	DIVIDEND	HIGH AND DATE		LOW AND DATE		CLOSE
3,102,700	American Can	$ 7.00	163½	Dec. 19	153½	Apr. 20	160
773,863	American Telephone	9.00	134¾	Dec. 18	121⅛	June 26	130½
172,100	Eastman Kodak	8.00	114⅞	Nov. 26	104⅛	Apr. 21	110⅞
2,623,365	General Electric	8.00	322	Dec. 3	193½	Jan. 3	320
593,900	General Motors	5.00	66⅞	Dec. 27	55¾	Oct. 15	65⅜
2,589,000	General Motors (old)	0	16¼	Feb. 1	12¾	May 20	15¼
251,300	Goodrich	0	38½	Dec. 30	17	June 19	37½
300,734	International Harvester	5.00	110½	Dec. 27	78	Jan. 3	107⅜
300,500	New York Air Brake	4.00	57	Dec. 29	36⅛	Apr. 22	55⅞
1,857,750	Standard Oil (N.J.)	1.00	42¼	Jan. 26	33	Apr. 14	40½
784,300	Union Pacific	10.00	151⅝	Dec. 18	126⅝	Mar. 3	149½
9,706,700	United States Steel	7.00	123	July 23	118⅜	Feb. 1	122⅝

SOURCE: *New York Times*, January 2, 1925.

Selected Common Stocks, 1925

VOLUME	STOCK	DIVIDEND	HIGH AND DATE		LOW AND DATE		CLOSE
6,814,252	American Can	$10.00	297⅜	Dec. 31	158⅛	Jan. 16	292½
569,367	American Telephone	9.00	145	Dec. 7	130⅝	Jan. 6	142⅝
450,100	Eastman Kodak	8.00	118	Jan. 19	104¾	July 18	111⅛
1,870,600	General Elec.	stock + 8.00	337¼	Aug. 24	227¼	Feb. 17	326
9,751,500	General Motors	12.00	149¾	Nov. 7	64⅝	Jan. 5	117½
1,468,450	Goodrich	4.00	74¾	Nov. 16	92	Jan. 3	97¾
1,147,700	International Harvester	5.00	138¼	Sept. 18	96⅛	Mar. 25	129⅞
358,800	New York Air Brake	2.00	56½	Jan. 2	31½	Sept. 17	37
2,991,990	Standard Oil (N.J.)	1.00	47½	Feb. 3	38⅜	Mar. 30	46
886,600	Union Pacific	10.00	153¼	Jan. 10	133¼	Apr. 24	150
12,243,700	United States Steel	7.00	139¼	Apr. 7	112⅛	May 7	126

SOURCE: *New York Times*, January 1, 1926.

first time, the Dow-Jones Industrials remained above the 100 level for the entire year. The extent of the rise has led some market historians to state that the bull market of the twenties began late in 1924, and ended five years later.

Dow-Jones Averages, 1918–1931

	INDUSTRIALS		RAILS	
YEAR	HIGH	LOW	HIGH	LOW
1918	89.07	73.38	92.91	77.21
1919	119.62	79.15	91.13	73.63
1920	109.88	66.75	85.37	67.83
1921	81.50	63.90	77.56	65.52
1922	103.43	78.59	93.99	74.43
1923	105.38	85.76	90.63	76.78
1924	120.51	88.33	99.50	80.23
1925	159.30	115.00	112.93	92.82
1926	166.64	135.20	123.23	102.41
1927	202.40	152.73	144.82	119.92
1928	300.00	191.23	152.70	132.60
1929	381.17	198.69	189.11	128.07
1930	294.07	157.71	157.94	91.65
1931	194.36	73.79	111.58	31.42

SOURCE: *Dow-Jones Investors' Handbook,* 1966, pp. 50–51.

The financial community greeted 1926 with confidence; even Noyes was willing to admit that there were few clouds in sight. Secretary Mellon, by now a major hero of the business community, promised further tax cuts and a balanced budget. The international scene was calmer than at any time since the end of the war, he believed, and this too augured well for American business. Writing for *The Times* on January 1, 1926, Mellon said:

The return of England and many other countries to the gold standard and the further progress made in the stabilization of exchanges during the year reflect substantial improvement in the world's affairs. The currency reforms effected are important steps in the gradual readjustment of economic conditions which were so largely dislocated during and following the war. With the working out of the Dawes Plan, the settlement of international debts, the reorganization of currency systems, and the stabilization of exchanges, many uncertainties have been removed, so that we are justified in concluding that the way is clear now for a more complete recovery.

The bull market ran out of steam in late February of 1926, however. Business was poor early in the year and many investors and speculators, believing prices had risen too fast in 1925, began to sell heavily. Stocks recovered somewhat in the summer of 1926, as the Poincaré government ended a financial crisis in France; they fell again in October, when the Florida land boom collapsed. In all, 1926 might be considered a stand-off year at worst and, at best, only the end of the first stage of the bull market.

From September 1924 to February 1926 the Dow-Jones Industrials had risen 37 per cent, the greatest and most sustained increase since the neutrality boom of 1915. In retrospect, we can see that March and April were consolidation and liquidation months, preceding the next step in the bull market, which began in late April and gathered steam toward the end of the year. Despite violent fluctuations, the general tone of the market remained good. There were many "zigs" and "zags," but the upward moves were generally stronger than the dips.

Selected Common Stocks, 1926

VOLUME	STOCK	DIVIDEND	HIGH AND DATE		LOW AND DATE		CLOSE
8,846,300	American Can	$2.00	63⅛	Aug. 4	38⅞	Mar. 30	49
606,090	American Telephone	9.00	151	Dec. 18	139⅝	June 18	149⅞
228,400	Eastman Kodak	8.00	136¾	Dec. 27	106⅝	Mar. 30	133
2,054,100	General Electric	3.00	95½	Aug. 14	79	June 6	83⅞
12,219,200	General Motors	11.00	173½	Oct. 2	137¼	Nov. 20	153¾
718,900	Goodrich	4.00	70¾	Feb. 3	39½	Nov. 30	43
1,242,100	International Harvester	6.00	158⅛	Dec. 15	112¼	Mar. 29	142½
353,700	New York Air Brake	3.00	46¾	July 3	36½	Jan. 2	43¼
3,314,400	Standard Oil (N.J.)	1.50	46⅜	Jan. 2	37⅜	Dec. 10	38¾
939,700	Union Pacific	10.00	168⅜	Oct. 1	141½	Mar. 30	162¼
25,252,600	United States Steel	7.00	160½	Dec. 17	117	Apr. 15	157⅜

SOURCE: *New York Times,* January 2, 1927.

Raskob set out for a short European vacation in the summer of 1926. At the time he told a market analyst that a recent rise in General Motors common was only to be expected, and that a further increase in the stock's value would soon follow. While it was true that General Motors was around the 189 mark, a record high, earnings were also zooming. "I am convinced the corporation will earn more than $35 a share this year," said Raskob. "When the former proportionate prices of Associated Dry Goods, American Can, and General Electric are compared as to earnings, General Motors, with earnings running at such a rate, is cheap at this price and should and will sell at least one hundred points higher." [6]

Almost as though in response to Raskob's interview, General Motors began to rise, reaching 225 in August just before the company was refinanced. After a stock dividend, G.M. continued to climb, influencing others as it went. Industrial news was bad toward the end of 1926, as the effects of a British recession were felt in America, but prices rose into 1927. To some, it seemed that the stock market had been cut loose from its economic moorings. And to a degree it was.

Corporation profits were $5.5 billion in 1927; in 1926 they had been $6.9 billion. Despite this decline, dividend payments rose from $4.6 billion to $4.9 billion. This meant that only $.6 billion were retained for expansion, against $2.3 billion in 1926. Depreciation charges were approximately $3.4 billion in both years. On the other hand, there is no indication that corporate expansion slowed down in the 1927 recession. The profit decline was compensated for by huge bond and stock flotations on Wall Street and bank borrowings, the impact of the Mellon tax cut, and Federal Reserve policy.

The capital markets were unusually active in 1927. Whereas in 1926 some $6.3 billion in stocks and bonds were floated—a postwar record—a new high was established in 1927, with $7.8 billion in new securities. Corporate bonded debt, $29 billion in 1926, rose to $35.2 billion in 1927. The market was able

6. Barron. *They Told Barron,* p. 113.

to sustain these heavy borrowings, and even more. In 1927 over twenty nations placed large bond issues with Wall Street houses. In addition, foreign corporations floated their securities in New York; Americans purchased some $800 million in both government and private foreign loans in 1927. This, in the face of an American business recession, which in previous times had led to a constriction in the capital markets. The reason for this change can be found in Federal Reserve actions.

The business recession led the Federal Reserve to reduce the rediscount rate to 3½ per cent, a move which resulted in lower rates across the board. In addition, the Federal Reserve was aggressive in its open market operations. Between July and December Reserve banks purchased $435 million worth of bonds, injecting that amount of new money into the economy. These moves, designed to stimulate a sluggish economy, succeeded in their objective.

Ordinarily, declines in profits will be signaled by or cause a market decline. In either case, usually there is a distinct connection between prices on Wall Street and the national economy. As indices declined in 1927, prices rose, going from 157.6 to 199.6. There were several reasons for this strange phenomenon.

In the first place, dividends *did* rise in 1927, indicating corporation leaders thought the economic decline was temporary and that they would risk their liquidity to back their beliefs. There had been economic irregularities earlier in the decade, and each was followed by a bull market. There was no reason to consider this dislocation any different than the others.

A second reason can be found in the monetary situation. The Federal Reserve's actions in lowering the rediscount rate, and the huge amounts of money available from investment trusts and other organizations, led to a lowering of the rate for brokers' loans, and not a raise as normally would have been the case. Call loans increased during 1927, at a more rapid rate than installment purchases or commercial loans. In the last six months of the year, loans and investments of member banks rose by almost $1.8 billion. Only 7 per cent of this amount went for commercial loans. Some was used for building and reserve funds, but a large amount found its way into the call money market. In this period, brokers' loans rose 24 per cent—a record up to that time.

Many observers charged that this was a natural result of the central bank's easy money policy. Governor Strong was roundly criticized on this account by economists H. Parker Willis, Benjamin M. Anderson, and others who argued against a rediscount cut. Strong's response was plausible and convincing, even though he did not come to grips with his critics. We had to lower the rate, he said, for several reasons:

1) To avoid a precipitous decline in the exchanges, especially sterling, which would weaken the bank position abroad. 2) To avoid restrictions upon our exports. 3) To avoid a chill to domestic business. 4) To avoid embarrassment to the smooth operation of the Dawes Plan. . . .[7]

What Strong was saying, in effect, was that the high tariff position of the twenties—combined with fear that business would collapse without a continued dose of easy money, and the inextricable ties of America to Europe's economies—forced these policies on the Federal Reserve System. Although he did not say so directly, Strong intimated that international collapse might have resulted had not the central bank gone along with the easy money advocates. The market rise, which grew out of this policy, was a natural concomitant of government and banking actions earlier in the decade.

All of this would have been incomprehensible to the "man in the street." As far as he was concerned, business was sound in 1927. Negotiations were well under way for the Kellogg-Briand Pact to outlaw war. The first talking motion picture was shown; Babe Ruth hit 60 home runs. And most important insofar as the buoyant optimism of the times was concerned, Charles A. Lindbergh flew solo from New York to Paris on

7. Lester Chandler. *Benjamin Strong: Central Banker* (Washington, 1958), pp. 461–62.

Selected Common Stocks, 1927

VOLUME	STOCK	DIVIDEND	HIGH AND DATE			LOW AND DATE			CLOSE
6,534,000	American Can	$ 2.00	77⅝	Dec.	20	43⅝	Mar.	31	75
1,058,100	American Telephone	9.00	185½	Oct.	11	149¼	Jan.	3	178⅝
347,300	Eastman Kodak	8.00	175¼	Sept.	20	126¼	Jan.	28	164¼
4,375,600	General Electric	5.00	146⅝	Sept.	7	81	Jan.	27	135¾
7,961,670	General Motors	6.00	141	Oct.	4	113¼	Aug.	19	138
1,792,400	Goodrich	4.00	96½	Dec.	7	42¾	Mar.	9	93½
2,063,500	International Harvester	6.00	255⅝	Dec.	22	135⅜	Jan.	18	244⅛
822,900	New York Air Brake	3.00	50	June	9	39¼	Oct.	25	46
2,528,500	Standard Oil (N.J.)	1.50	41⅜	Feb.	5	35⅛	Apr.	29	39¾
966,300	Union Pacific	10.00	197¾	Dec.	3	159½	Jan.	27	191¾
16,935,300	United States Steel	7.00	160½	Sept.	16	111⅜	Jan.	28	151⅞

SOURCE: *New York Times,* January 2, 1928.

May 20–21. All of these events—even Ruth's baseball prowess —sparked bull drives on Wall Street. Wright Aeronautical, a firm associated with Lindbergh's *Spirit of St. Louis,* soared from 25 to 245 in the nineteen months that followed the flight. Seaboard Airlines, a coastal railroad, rose on heavy volume because speculators thought it to be involved with airplanes.

The spectacular market advance of 1927, which saw volume expand almost 128 million shares over the 1926 figure, was a banner year for the Wall Street community. Everything seemed to rise—including the value of a stock exchange seat, the

Prices of Seats on the New York Stock Exchange, 1920–1927

YEAR	HIGH	LOW
1920	$115,000	$ 85,000
1921	100,000	77,500
1922	100,000	86,000
1923	100,000	76,000
1924	101,000	76,000
1925	150,000	99,000
1926	175,000	133,000
1927	310,000	175,000

SOURCE: *New York Times,* January 2, 1928.

worth of which was determined by the volume of trades and the inside information to which seatholders were privy. Once again, year-end forecasts were optimistic, as business leaders and market analysts agreed the boom would continue into 1928. There were some voices of caution, but not many. One of these belonged to conservative banker Eugene Meyer, who began putting his customers into high-grade utility and government bonds. When asked why, Meyer responded, "What will happen if they forget to bid?"

8

Problems and Perspectives: 1928

BY JANUARY 1928 there was a general sentiment on Wall Street that stock prices had risen too high, too fast. At the same time a lull was noted in the economy, caused in part by the Ford conversion from the Model "T" to the Model "A," [1] and a prolonged European slump. Investment services ran ads asking, "Will you Overstay the Bull Market?" and "Is the Process of Deflation Underway?" Senator La Follette introduced a resolution to limit the Federal Reserve's powers in granting loans which were destined for use in the call money market. The Harvard Economic Society thought that "business was entering upon a period of temporary readjustment," and the Committee on Economic Changes noted with disapproval certain weaknesses in the nation's economic structure. Moody's Investment Service, one of the most respected voices on Wall Street, warned that stock prices were too high, having "over-discounted anticipated progress." Years later Bernard Baruch and Joseph Kennedy confided that they began to sell stocks in January 1928. Baruch started buying gold from Alaska

1. Ford's conversion from the Model "T" to the Model "A" was one of the more dramatic incidents of the decade. Faced with hot competition from General Motors' Chevrolet Division, Ford decided to put out an entirely new car in 1927. He shut down production for six months while the conversion took place, and late in the year unveiled his new automobile. Although a popular model, the "A" was unable to defeat the Chevrolet in the 1930s. Ford had produced 56 per cent of the nation's autos in 1921; in the conversion year of 1927, he turned out only 9.3 per cent of the new cars.

Juneau Mines,[2] and told friends to watch the economic statistics with care, for a crash might be in the making. Stock prices did break sharply in January, ending the long bull market which had begun in April 1926.

The decline was short-lived. After leveling off in February, prices rose on a surge of buying in early March, wiping out the January-February losses and setting new all-time highs along the way. The last and most spectacular stage of the bull market was under way.

On March 24, Raskob spoke to reporters before setting off on his annual European trip. He scoffed at the notion that stock prices were inflated and out of control. At the moment General Motors was selling for 187; Raskob said it should be higher, at least 225. G.M. gained 5 points the next trading day and 7 the following one. G.M. reached 224¾, just a shade below the Raskob projection, on November 7.

Selected Common Stocks, 1928

VOLUME	STOCK	DIVIDEND	HIGH AND DATE		LOW AND DATE		CLOSE
11,422,000	American Can	$ 4.00	117½	Dec. 16	70⅛	Jan. 18	110⅜
1,510,100	American Telephone	9.00	211	May 17	172	July 24	193
384,800	Eastman Kodak	8.00	194¼	July 30	163	Mar. 20	183
6,497,200	General Electric	6.00	221½	Dec. 31	124	Feb. 27	221½
43,880,400	General Motors	9.50	224¾	Nov. 7	130	Jan. 10	203¾
2,715,100	Goodrich	4.00	109¼	Dec. 28	68½	June 18	103½
262,900	New York Air Brake	3.00	50½	Feb. 10	37⅞	Oct. 22	44⅛
6,226,300	Standard Oil (N.J.)	1.50	59⅜	Nov. 30	37¾	Feb. 18	55
835,800	Union Pacific	10.00	224⅞	Nov. 12	186½	Feb. 6	218½
19,809,700	United States Steel	7.00	172½	Nov. 16	132⅜	June 25	151¼

SOURCE: *New York Times,* January 2, 1929.

Although the bullish surge was welcomed by speculators and viewed by many as a sign of American economic vitality, Benjamin Strong and others at the Federal Reserve were con-

2. Traditionally, speculators and investors will purchase gold or gold mining shares when they believe the price of common stocks will fall. This is done in the belief that when all else has lost its value, gold will still be in demand. As a result, the gold price and quotations for gold shares are important *contracyclical* indicators.

cerned that the market was getting out of hand. Strong was a firm believer in the power of his bank and was convinced that a rise in the rediscount rate combined with open market operations could dampen speculation any time he and his colleagues thought it wise to use them. Such moves might cause America's economic growth to slow down and be harmful to international liquidity but, when and if necessary, he would act. The March bull market convinced him that the moment had come. Strong raised the New York rate from 3½ to 4 per cent that spring, then to 4½ per cent, and finally to 5 per cent late in the year. At the same time the New York bank initiated aggressive open market operations, selling $300 million worth of bonds in the first half of the year so as to dry up the money supply. Other Reserve banks followed his lead, and commercial banks were obliged to raise their rates in sympathy. As Strong knew it would, the price of call money rose sharply, hitting 10 per cent by year's end. But Strong's much-vaunted automatic controls failed to work. Although member banks reduced their call loan commitments, the total amount of such loans rose steadily, from $4.4 billion at the end of 1927 to $6.4 billion a year later.

The source of this new money was no secret: it came from the corporations and individuals who benefited from the bull market, and over whom the Federal Reserve had no control.

By mid-1928 many corporations felt security prices were too high, and looked for safe investments returning high rates of interest. As the rates for brokers' loans rose, this market began to attract corporate capital. In many ways it was a perfect investment. The loans were secured; they were in demand; they paid high rates of interest; they were easily liquidated; and they supported the market prices of stocks in the very corporations making the loans. On the other hand, the situation was dangerous and illusory. Each market was feeding the other, with no new goods or services produced—just an aura of wealth. For example, an automobile company might borrow money to produce more cars, thus making larger profits which in the end would send the price of its stock upward. By 1928 such a company might wonder why it should take this route to prosperity. The new plant might show a return of 15 per cent if all went well, while the same amount of money invested in brokers' loans would return 10 per cent with no risk. Since the loans would be used to purchase stocks, including automobile issues, the company's securities would rise as much, if not more, as they would have had the money been invested in plant and equipment. Faced with this kind of logic, the companies entered the call money market.

Brokers' Loans by Selected Companies, 1929

COMPANY	AMOUNT
Electric Bond and Share	$157,579,000
Bethlehem Steel	157,450,000
Standard Oil (N.J.)	97,824,000
Tri-Continental	62,150,000
Chrysler	60,150,000
Cities Service	41,900,000
Anaconda Copper	32,500,000
American & Foreign Power	30,321,000
General Motors	25,000,000

SOURCE: Ferdinand Lundberg. *America's 60 Families* (New York, 1937), p. 221.

Wealthy individuals and firms also entered this market. Pierre du Pont had $32 million invested in brokers' loans at one time, and Morgan & Company, eschewing its reputation for conservatism, put nearly $110 million in call loans. Such companies and individuals more than negated any action Strong and his colleagues at the Federal Reserve might take.

Strong died in October 1928 and did not see the result of such investments, but he warned of them before his death. His successor, George Harrison, seemed content to continue his policies for the most part.

President Coolidge was apprised of what was happening, but he did little to curb speculation. When told of the rise in brokers' loans, the President opined that it was the result of a "natural expansion of business" in which he could see "nothing

Brokers' Loans by Source, 1927–1929 (in millions)

DATE	NEW YORK BANKS	OUTSIDE BANKS	OTHERS	TOTAL
Dec. 31, 1927	$1,550	$1,050	$1,830	$4,430
June 30, 1928	1,080	960	2,860	4,900
Dec. 31, 1928	1,640	915	3,885	6,440
Oct. 4, 1929	1,095	760	6,640	8,525

SOURCE: Chandler. *Benjamin Strong,* p. 426.

unfavorable." Later on, however, he told H. Parker Willis, editor-in-chief of the *Journal of Commerce,* that he considered "any loan made for gambling in stocks 'excessive.' " When Willis pleaded with Coolidge to say so publicly, the President demurred. "Well, I regard myself as the representative of the government and not as an individual. When technical matters come up I feel called on to refer them to the proper department of the government which has some information about them and then, unless there is some good reason, I use this information as a basis for whatever I have to say; but that does not prevent me from thinking what I please as an individual."

Then in the last year of his administration, Coolidge wished to do nothing to ruin what he considered an excellent record. The President was never known for aggressive actions; he would not change at this stage of his career. In his State of the Union message of December 4, 1928, "Silent Cal" assured his listeners that "No Congress of the United States ever assembled, on surveying the state of the Union, has met with a more pleasing prospect than that which appears at the present time. In the domestic field there is tranquility and contentment . . . and the highest record of years of prosperity. In the foreign field there is peace, the goodwill which comes from mutual under-standing. . . ." The outgoing President's message was simple, as was his conclusion: "Regard the present with satisfaction and anticipate the future with optimism."

Coolidge's private thoughts differed from his public pro-nouncements. A few months later he declined to accept the

G.O.P. nomination for another term, although he could have
had it without too much difficulty. Instead, he allowed the
Hoover boom to grow, saying nothing to encourage his own sup-
porters. Grace Coolidge was asked why her husband wanted
to leave the White House. Her answer was direct. "Poppa says
there's a depression coming."

Federal Reserve Chairman Roy Young was more outspoken.
In February 1929, as Coolidge prepared to leave the White
House, Young issued two warnings against excessive speculation. Unless private banks curbed their brokers' loans still
further, he said, the Federal Reserve would be obliged to take
action. Young threw down the gauntlet to the banking community; it was picked up by Charles Mitchell.

As head of the National City Bank as well as a director of
the New York Federal Reserve Bank, Mitchell was one of the
most powerful individuals in American finance. An incurable
optimist and bull as well as one deep in speculation himself,
Mitchell had a philosophical and personal involvement in the
surging market. His voice was clear in response to Young's
threats. If and when the Federal Reserve attempted to curb
lending, he would advance $25 million to traders. "We feel
that we have an obligation which is paramount to any Federal
Reserve warning," said Mitchell, "or anything else, to avert
any dangerous crisis in the money market." Professor of Economics Joseph Stagg Lawrence, speaking from Princeton,
applauded Mitchell's statement and pledge, and attacked Young
for having "undertaken a punitive excursion against the stock
market without adequate provocation and in contravention of
every principle of justice." Perhaps it is time, said Lawrence,
for the New York banks to declare their independence from the
Federal Reserve System, an outmoded institution forced upon
the business community by antique reformers. "Although the
provinces dominate in politics there is no reason why that do-
minion should extend into the field of finance."

So the battle was joined, with the forces of control challenging those which claimed market prices were an accurate reflection of economic realities. The former group observed that more than $11.3 billion was added to stock values in 1928, after a slightly lower increase in 1927. The Gross National Product in both years averaged around $90 billion, while capital formation was slightly less than $17 billion on the average. In the face of these figures, it seemed unreasonable to expect the large firms listed on the New York Stock Exchange—which represented less than half the nation's productive force and almost none of its agricultural produce—to show such a rise.

The bulls responded by saying that their critics did not understand the dynamism of the American economy or the mechanics of the market. In the past, they said, stock prices reflected the present because the future was uncertain. Now, however, the nation was enjoying permanent prosperity; depressions were no longer possible. If you *knew* that a company's earnings were increasing at a rate of 20 per cent a year, then it was clear they would double in less than five years if compounded. Would it not be wise to take these anticipated earnings into consideration? In the past, stocks sold at ten times earnings. The stock which sold at fifteen times earnings in 1928 was, in reality, selling at less than eight times 1933 earnings, and so was more conservative a purchase than it would have been a decade earlier! The market rise, concluded the more articulate bulls, was not based on fantasy, but on a more realistic and contemporary view of the economy than that held by their

General Motors Common Stock, 1925–1928

YEAR	HIGH	LOW	EARNINGS PER SHARE	DIVI-DEND	SHARES OUT-STANDING	CAR PRODUCTION
1925	149¾	64⅝	$21.00	$12.00	5,161,599	835,902
1926	173½	137¼	20.53	11.00	8,700,000	1,234,850
1927	141	113¼	12.99	6.00	17,400,000	1,562,748
1928	224¾	130	15.35	9.50	17,400,000	1,810,806

SOURCE: *New York Times,* 1925–1929.

opponents. Their assertions could be illustrated by a study of General Motors, a bellwether stock [3] of 1928.

On an adjusted basis,[4] General Motors' earnings rose from $21 to more than $46 from 1925 to 1928, and dividends from $12 to more than $29. In 1928, G.M. common sold for a high of 224¾, approximately fifteen times earnings. At that rate, G.M. would be earning almost $100 a share by 1931, paying a dividend of some $70. In terms of the 1928 price, this was 2¼ times earnings for a return of well over 25 per cent! Who could say, then, that G.M.'s 1928 high was out of line with realities? In fact, the price should be much higher, said the bulls, and in 1929 they did send it up again.

Similar statements could be made about other stocks, all of which were high priced by 1920 standards, but reasonable by the rationale of 1929. Indeed, by today's methods of valuation, some 1928 prices were low, as they would be at the height of the 1929 bull market. Consider the following comparisons between the 1929 and 1962 highs, both of which preceded sharp market declines:

Prices and Earnings of Selected Issues, 1929 and 1962

STOCK	1929 HIGH AND EARNINGS		1962 HIGH AND EARNINGS*	
American Can	184½	$ 8.02	47½	$2.81
Eastman Kodak	264¾	9.57	55¼	1.73
General Electric	403	8.97	78½	2.97
Goodrich	105¾	4.87	72½	2.87
International Harvester	142	7.11	31⅝	2.13
Standard Oil (N.J.)	83	4.75	76⅝	4.74
United States Steel	198¾	21.19	57½	3.30

* adjusted
SOURCES: *New York Times,* 1929 and *Moody's Handbook,* 1967.

3. A *bellwether stock* is one whose activities are considered especially meaningful to the Wall Street community. In the 1920s, General Motors, R.C.A., and American Telephone & Telegraph were considered bellwether stocks.
4. In order to better understand and appreciate a stock's progress,

One could say that in 1929 the prices for American Can, General Electric, Goodrich, and International Harvester were unrealistically high by present standards, while those for Eastman Kodak, Standard Oil of New Jersey, and U. S. Steel were not. It might also be observed that Goodrich, General Electric, and International Harvester were considered glamour stocks in 1929, and so were afforded higher price/earnings ratios than most other issues. Even with this, they sold at between twenty and thirty times earnings. Today's glamour stocks—Syntex, Litton, I.B.M., Polaroid, Fairchild Camera, etc.—usually sell for fifty times earnings and sometimes beyond that.

To illustrate this point, we might consider the record of Radio Corporation of America, the greatest glamour issue of the twenties, and compare it with Syntex, a similar favorite of the post–World War II market. There are differences, to be sure. R.C.A.'s position in its market was more secure than that of Syntex in birth control and other drug fields. Still, R.C.A.'s prices in the twenties were lower than those of Syntex in recent years.

Comparison of R.C.A. and Syntex Common Stocks for Selected Years

YEAR	HIGH R.C.A.	EARNINGS (SHARE)	YEAR	HIGH SYNTEX	EARNINGS (SHARE)
1925	77⅞	$ 1.32	1962	11	$0.14
1926	61⅝	2.85	1963	67½	0.47
1927	101	6.15	1964	95¼	0.91
1928	420	15.98	1965	109	1.18

SOURCES: *New York Times* and *Moody's Handbook,* 1967.

At the height of the 1929 bull market, and after a five-for-one split, R.C.A. sold for 114¾, showing earnings of $1.58 for

---

analysts will attempt to calculate its growth by adjusting for stock splits, stock dividends, rights offerings, and so forth. Thus, a stock which earned $2.00 a share when 1 million shares were outstanding, may report $2.00 a share a decade later, when through stock splits and the like the capitalization has risen to 10 million shares. In such a case, the company may be said to have earned $20 a share on an *adjusted basis.*

the year. In contrast, Syntex sold for 109 with earnings of $1.18 in 1965.

Similarly, it is difficult to argue that dividends were low in relation to prices in 1928. Many issues sold at prices so high that they returned less than 3 per cent, but it was still possible to obtain 4 per cent and more on good-quality stocks. In addition, dividends, like earnings, were on the rise in 1928, making lower yields more bearable. Finally, many companies issued rights in the late twenties, entitling stockholders to purchase additional shares at prices lower than those quoted on Wall Street. In some cases, the rights were more valuable than the dividends. One is drawn to the conclusion, then, that dividends, like price/earnings ratios, were unreasonable in 1928–1929 only when compared with those of 1920 and earlier; when placed side by side with those of today, they appear sensible and even a bit on the low side.

Prices and Dividends of Selected Issues, *1928 and 1966*

STOCK	1928 HIGH AND DIVIDEND		1966 HIGH AND DIVIDEND	
Allied Chemical	253¾	$ 6.00	50⅛	$1.85
American Can	117½	4.00	59¾	2.20
American Smelting & Refining	285	8.00	82⅜	3.30
American Tobacco	184⅞	8.00	40⅝	1.80
Chrysler	140½	3.00	61⅜	2.00
General Electric	221½	6.00	120	2.60
International Harvester	394¾	10.00	52⅞	1.73
Sears Roebuck	197½	2.50	65¾	1.15
Union Carbide	209	6.00	70⅜	2.00

SOURCES: *New York Times,* January 2, 1929 and *Moody's Handbook,* 1967.

Naturally, there were differences, many of them major, between the bull market of the twenties and that of the sixties. There was no Securities and Exchange Commission in 1929 as there is today; the policeman is on the corner. Margin buying is less common now than in the twenties. The institutions [5] are more powerful and have on several occasions supported the market in a way they either failed to do or could not do in 1929. In 1962 the average daily volume was 3,818,000 shares; in 1929 the figure was 4,277,000. But there were only 1,127,-700,000 shares listed in 1929 against 7,659,200,000 in 1962. Thus, the turnover rate in the earlier year was 119 per cent while in 1962 it was only 13 per cent. Nor was 1929 unusual in this respect. The boom and panic year of 1907 saw a turnover rate of 160 per cent, while in 1901 the figure was 319 per cent, a record which will remain for a long time. Was 1929 a hectic year on Wall Street? The figures can be used to support both a negative and positive answer to this question.

We may say, then, that although stock prices were high in 1928 and 1929, this must be accepted in the context of 1920 values and not those of the present. The most dangerous problem was the absence of safeguards and conservative institutions on Wall Street. One might conclude that the flaws in the 1928–1929 bull market were not quantitative—the prices of the stocks—but qualitative—the nature of the market's institutions and how they operated. Had the high prices been arrived at without the use of brokers' loans, without participation in the market by large corporations, without the unbridled irresponsibility of the men who had become the Street's leaders, with a stronger and more respected Federal Reserve System, and with the Securities and Exchange Commission or something like it, the situation would not have been critical.

There were some who realized the weaknesses of the market. President-elect Hoover, who said, "Our whole business system would break down in a day if there was not a high sense of moral responsibility in our business world," recognized the signs of a break, and he spoke against speculation and excesses. Later on he would say there was little he could do. The New York Stock

5. When Wall Streeters speak of institutions, they usually mean the large pension funds, mutual funds, and other important holders of securities.

Exchange and other exchanges were incorporated in New York; only the governor of that state could take actions against speculation. Governor Franklin D. Roosevelt, in Albany for a few months, remained quiet about the Wall Street situation, however. Senator Carter Glass of Virginia, father of the Federal Reserve System, called for strong curbs on the New York banking community and Mitchell's resignation from the Federal Reserve Board, but nothing came of this. At year-end some businessmen gave hints of future problems. Arthur Lehman of Lehman Brothers thought there might be troubles ahead. "When I say that the outlook for business is doubtful, I mean it literally, and not euphemistically, as predicting bad business," he said. "Production has been at a high rate during the past year and it is difficult to see where in many lines an expansion could take place." Willis H. Booth, vice president of the Guaranty Trust, thought, "The business outlook is satisfactory—not that everything is exactly as it should be; it never is. Most industries are doing well and promise better. Wages are high." Alexander Dana Noyes remained skeptical. In his year-end review, he concluded:

Conservative judgement has only past experience to guide it; but the rather uniform teaching of that experience is that an era of violent speculation for the rise begins, like that which began at the end of 1924, in abnormally easy money; that in due time, if continued, it converts the comfortable credit situation into one of great stringency; that speculation ignores the high money rates, willingly paying the price demanded for credit procured from unusual sources; but that these abnormal facilities suddenly fail it in the end—conservative prophets seem as yet to be puzzled over the evidence of 1928 to make categorical predictions.

Noyes also admitted, however, that those who had followed his advice earlier had missed out on huge profits in the bull market. *The Times* analyst was contradicted by his own financial page writers, who viewed dips such as those of January-February and the sharp fall in early December as mere interludes in the bull market. In an unsigned article of December 21, 1928, a *Times* writer said:

The underlying strength of the stock market, which brought sharp gains yesterday in many individual issues, has been about as much a surprise to Wall Street as was the recent decline. The professional element of the Street has been certain that a "secondary reaction" of large proportions would follow in the wake of the sharp decline, and on this theory a sizable short interest has been built up in the market. Most of these short sales now show a loss, and short covering furnished a considerable part of yesterday's business. Many more brokerage houses are hopping nimbly over to the bull side of the market, and once again yesterday many tips were in circulation. No one predicted, however, that the market would start out once more in a burst of wild excitement, but professional opinion is that the mid-December crash was a "reaction in a bull market" rather than "the end of speculative frenzy."

The lesson of mid-December was "Don't sell America short." As *The Times* writer indicated, the bears were switching in the light of their obvious failure to crack the strong bull market.

There were many more who thought the advance would persist, and their voices drowned out those of the timid. Charles Mitchell said, "Business is entering the New Year upon a high level of activity and with confidence in the continuation of prosperity." To be sure, there were weaknesses visible in some parts of the economy, but these would straighten themselves out with little difficulty. "No complaint regarding the level of stock prices, however, is justified except from the standpoint of credit strain," was Mitchell's conclusion. Thomas Watson of I.B.M. said, "We may look with confidence to the progress of business in 1929," and Lewis Pierson of the Irving Trust thought, "All major indicators point to a prosperous coming year." *Time* seemed to agree, naming Walter P. Chrysler "Man of the Year," and publisher Henry Luce and his staff were preparing to bring out a new magazine, *Fortune,* which would be dedicated to the proposition and the "generally accepted commonplace that America's great achievement has been Business."

As predicted, the market moved upward early in the year, buoyed by massive buying of and by the investment trusts and optimistic statements from Wall Street, the universities, and

Washington. Rumors were spread that Cutten, the Fisher brothers, Livermore, and others were forming bull pools to back selected stocks. To be sure, there were several sharp corrections, but each time the bulls moved in, along with shorts covering their sales, to lift prices once more. The market was an exciting place that spring and summer, but also dangerous.

In early spring Paul Warburg, the ancient leader of Kuhn, Loeb, spoke of market conditions. Warburg had lived through the 1907 panic, and now he saw the same signals. Prices were too high, he said. The market rise was "quite unrelated to respective increases in plant, property, or earning power." The "colossal volume of loans" had reached "a saturation point." Unless "the orgy of unrestrained speculation" was ended, a crash would surely follow, and then would come "a general depression involving the entire country." Warburg was accused of "sandbagging American prosperity."

Exchange President E. H. H. Simmons was also worried. "Speculation in securities may not be a bad thing in itself," he thought. "It is, however, necessary to recognize that we may have too much or too little security speculation. . . ." But his hands were tied: "The New York Stock Exchange is not itself concerned with the course of security prices, so long as these prices result from fair, free, and open markets."

Were the markets fair, free, and open? By midsummer manipulations were no longer conducted secretly; everyone seemed to know when and how certain stocks were lifted up and then let go. Market letters wrote of U. S. Steel being "taken in hand" on Tuesday morning, and R.C.A. "at 1:30 tomorrow." The "Old Counselor," really a University of Chicago professor, appeared on radio to offer advice on stocks, and he was followed by millions. Baruch recommended stock purchases while secretly selling his holdings. "The bears have no mansions on Fifth Avenue," he told one reporter. Later on, Baruch would write: "When beggars and shoeshine boys, barbers and beauticians can tell you how to get rich it is time to remind yourself that there is no more dangerous illusion than the belief that one can get something for nothing."

Noyes and Roger Babson continued to warn of overspeculation, but Professor Charles Dice of Ohio State, in his *New Levels in the Stock Market,* thought quotations were "only registering the tremendous changes that were in progress." Joseph Davis of Stanford and Edmund Day of the University of Michigan became advisors for investment trusts. Irving Fisher's evenings were spent giving speeches to business groups on his theories of permanent prosperity. The Harvard Economic Society, slightly bearish in the beginning of 1929, joined the bulls at midyear. Never before had the university and college community been so engaged in such worldly matters. In 1929 the leading economists of Harvard, Yale, Princeton, Ohio State, Michigan—one can hardly think of a major institution missing from the list—were enrolled believers of the bull market.

Summer drew to an end with no sign of weakness on Wall Street. When the Federal Reserve raised the rediscount rate to 6 per cent in August, stocks only rose higher, disregarding all attempts to curb the boom. The boardrooms of large brokerages were jammed with speculators and people who did not own stocks, but were curious about the excitement. The atmosphere was lighthearted and carefree. A year earlier individuals who had made fortunes on Wall Street were applauded; now they were commonplace. Speculators, both large and small, were beginning to accept continued advances as an expected occurrence. Not even a rise in margin requirements made by some brokers could dampen the enthusiasm. The *Saturday Evening Post* printed a poem to illustrate this feeling:

Oh, hush thee, my babe, granny's bought some more shares
Daddy's gone out to play with the bulls and the bears,
Mother's buying on tips, and she simply can't lose,
And baby shall have some expensive new shoes!

On September 1 *The Times,* convinced of the underlying strength of the market, wrote:

One of the most striking features of the present chapter in Stock Market history is the failure of the trading community to take serious alarm at portents which once threw Wall Street into a state of alarm bordering on demoralization. In particular, the recent disregard of the succession of "smashed high records" for brokers' loans astonishes the older school of market operators. Undoubtedly the heavy margins required of traders by the commission houses have done much to build up this assurance. Traders who would formerly have taken the precaution of reducing their commitments just in case a reaction should set in, now feel confident that thay can ride out any storm which may develop. But more particularly, the repeated demonstrations which the market has given of its ability to "come back" with renewed strength after a sharp reaction has engendered a spirit of indifference to all the old time warnings. As to whether this attitude may not sometime itself become a danger-signal, Wall Street is not agreed.

9

The Crash

~~~~~~

AUGUST 20, 1929 was an important day for Wall Street analysts. Stocks rose briskly throughout the list, posting new highs as they went. At 2:00 P.M. the rails and utilities took fire, and for the rest of the session dominated trading. The next day the *Wall Street Journal* wrote:

Stocks derived further powerful impetus on the up side yesterday from the establishment of simultaneous, new highs in the Dow-Jones industrial and rail averages on Monday's close. According to the Dow theory, this development re-establishes the major upward trend. Reassurance on this score gave fresh stimulus to bullish enthusiasm, and a long list of representative stocks surged upward to new highs. . . . The outlook for the fall months seems brighter than at any time in recent years.

There were few difficulties on the international scene in late August and early September. The *Times* headline of September 1 was ARABS INVADE PALESTINE FROM THREE DIRECTIONS; FIGHT REPORTED AT HAIFA, but this was hardly of monumental importance to the United States of that day. On the same date, the newspapers ran stories assessing Hoover's first half year in the White House. "The 'engineering mind' applied to national government and international affairs has shown it can produce results in a new way," an article concluded, noting that "the real test of its political strength is yet to come." Still, Hoover was credited with maintaining confidence, and so was considered a bullish factor for Wall Street.

Stocks opened September on high ground and, in addition,

benefited from dividend increases and rights offerings. Indeed, the New York Stock Exchange itself, perhaps influenced by corporate practices, declared a dividend of a quarter membership to each seatholder, thus creating 275 new seats and bringing the total to 1,375. Like stocks, the price of an Exchange seat zoomed, hitting an all-time high of $625,000.

Had the newspaper reader of September 2 turned to the financial page—and most did—he would see few dark spots; only a handful of stocks were selling closer to their lows than highs.

Selected Stock Closings, September 1, 1929

STOCK	HIGH TO DATE	LOW TO DATE	SEPT. 1 PRICE	DIVIDEND
Adams Express	750	389	591	$ 6.00
Air Reduction	216¾	95⅛	214	3.00
Allis Chalmers	330	166	311½	7.00
American Car & Foundry	106½	92	98⅞	6.00
Chesapeake & Ohio	277½	195	277	10.00
Coca-Cola	154½	120⅝	152½	4.00
Consolidated Gas	182	95½	180¾	3.00
Famous-Players-Lasky	74	55½	72	3.00
Homestake Mining	93	72	80	7.00
Lorillard	31½	20	25⅝	0
Woolworth	100⅞	85	99¼	2.40

SOURCE: *New York Times,* September 2, 1929.

But prices fell on September 4, in what the *Journal* called "the first technical correction of importance." Some brokers advised switches from speculative stocks to bonds; others raised the price of call money and margin requirements. Then prices rallied, and on September 11 the *Journal* reported:

Price movements in the main body of stocks yesterday continued to display the characteristics of a major advance temporarily halted for technical readjustment. Trading was marked by intermittent selling waves, demonstrating that the process of correction was still uncompleted.

It was an unusually hot September. Theater managers reported poor ticket sales, even for the "talkies." Connie Mack's

Philadelphia Athletics, powered by Mickey Cochrane and Jimmy Foxx, took the championship, four games to one, from Joe McCarthy's Chicago Cubs, led by Hack Wilson and Rogers Hornsby. And while the nation followed the series, went to the beaches, purchased fall clothing, and reflected on permanent prosperity, the stock market started to show signs of weakness.

By the end of the month Adams Express was down to 530; Westinghouse had fallen from 288 to 233. Most losses were slight, such as Continental Can's 4-point decline from 92 and Air Reduction's 13-point slide from 216. In fact, there were almost as many gains as losses. J. I. Case, a speculative favorite, closed the month at 399 for a 45-point advance; U. S. Rubber added 5 points to its September opening of 47. But there were increased margin calls and news of declines in steel production, freight car loadings, and housing. On September 20, Clarence Hatry, an English speculator and businessman, declared bankruptcy in London; his industrial empire of photographic supplies, vending machines, and loan offices was soon shown to have been made possible through the forging of stocks and the issuance of unauthorized shares. This bad news was balanced, however, by reports that brokers' loans were still plentiful at 10 per cent. Even at this rate demand was high; the September increase alone was a record $670 million. The new investment trust, Lehman Corporation, was quoted at a 30 per cent premium soon after its first offering on September 20, the day of the Hatry collapse.

The advance became spotty during the last week in September and ended abruptly at the beginning of the new month. Then, on October 3, the market collapsed, in the worst selloff of the year to that date. Many newspapers carried the story on their front pages. Margin calls went out, and financial analysts wrote that the bull market might be coming to an end. Some brokerages began publishing lists of conservative issues for investment, suggesting that their customers consider yield and price/earnings ratios more carefully in the future. But others repeated the now-familiar statements that price/earnings ratios of twenty to one were not unreasonable in the 1929 market; that the investment trusts and "big boys" were waiting for the proper moment to purchase stocks—a time when "suckers" sold in panic; that bull pools were forming throughout the district; and that there was no reason to consider 60 per cent margin accounts as speculative. Arthur Cutten, who was said to have switched to the bear side of the market, took great pains to deny this. The *Journal* reported that "Mr. Cutten said no relaxation of the national prosperity was in sight, and expressed the opinion that the market structure could support brokers' loans of $10 billion to $12 billion."

Prices recovered on October 4, and the upward swing resumed. By the end of the week most issues showed sizable gains, especially U. S. Steel, R.C.A., Westinghouse, and General Electric, stocks which had "glamour" in 1929. The October 12 issue of the *Journal* proclaimed:

In the way of news developments, bulls have had much the best of it over the last week or so, and this, perhaps, is the main reason why the market has been able to score such a quick comeback. A week ago you heard all over the Street pessimistic forecasts as to the future of the market. You read in a number of newspapers . . . to the effect that we were in a major bear market. Stocks are now 10, 20, and 30 points above where they were a week ago, and optimism again prevails.

Others were of the same opinion. Charles Mitchell, still deep in speculation, told reporters, "I see no reason for the end-of-the-year slump which some people are predicting." Irving Fisher, who by this time had constructed "the Fisher Index" of stock prices and was spending most of his days away from Harvard in order to follow the market more closely, thought prices would be "a good deal higher than . . . today within a few months." Despite these and other optimistic statements, the markets opened lower on Monday morning, October 14, and proceeded to fall all week, ending with a partial collapse on Friday, when key issues lost five points or more. The decline continued into the half-day trading on Saturday, toward the end of which wholesale dumping took place.

Selected Common Stocks, October 14–19, 1929

STOCK	OCT. 14	OCT. 15	OCT. 16	OCT. 17	OCT. 18	OCT. 19
American Can	175¼	173⅝	166¾	169⅝	167	156
American Telephone	299½	295⅜	284	291½	286⅝	281¾
Eastman Kodak	243	242	231½	237¼	230⅛	217½
General Electric	368	361	349	354⅞	348½	339¼
General Motors	65¼	65⅜	64	64½	62½	60¼
Goodrich	68½	69½	67	65¾	64½	63
International Harvester	113⅝	111½	109⅜	112¾	106	105
New York Air Brake	45	45¾	46	46¼	46	45⅞
Standard Oil (N.J.)	80	80¼	79⅞	81¾	78	77
Union Pacific	270	274	270¾	268¼	266	263¼
United States Steel	227½	223⅛	213½	218½	211¼	209

SOURCE: *New York Times,* October 15-20, 1929.

The sharp decline of October 14–19 did not cause a panic; it was no worse than bearish weeks in previous years, and after each of these the market had recovered. Some thought the collapse was caused by a struggle between Livermore's bear pool and Cutten's bullish group. There were rumors that the investment trusts had depressed prices in the hope of causing large-scale selling by small investors, after which they would come in and pick up stocks at bargain prices. Fisher thought it merely the "shaking out of the lunatic fringe," and even Noyes believed the decline was about over, terming it a "correction."

Six million shares were traded on Monday, October 21. Although many blue chips were firm, the glamour stocks slumped badly, leading to renewed calls for "more margin!" The *Journal* remained optimistic. "There is a vast amount of money awaiting investment," was its comment on the Monday trading. "Thousands of traders and investors have been waiting for an opportunity to buy stocks on just such a break as has occurred over the last several weeks, and this buying, in time, will change the trend of the market." The newspaper was quickly vindicated: prices rose across the board on Tuesday morning—but then they fell back during the afternoon. The Wednesday opening was slow, as brokers remained wary, waiting to see which way the market would go. Then, in mid-morning, several key issues slumped on heavy volume. The decline spread through the rest of the list. Formerly blasé brokers, who had scoffed at talk of a major decline, tried to maintain their dignity while shouting offers to sell at two or three points below the previous transaction. And when no one appeared to buy, the shouts grew louder, and prices fell lower. Although there was no panic as yet, most brokers were nervous by the end of trading. Paper declines of more than $4 billion were registered that day. Case fell 46 points and Adams Express 96. Speculative issues generally suffered huge losses, while many blue chips dropped five points or more. Investment trusts showed the greatest declines; the leverage which in the past had operated to exaggerate gains, now worked to magnify losses.

As the clerks and runners labored late that night to ready the brokerages for the next morning, bankers met to discuss the day's events. It was generally agreed that the list was undergoing its most serious correction of the decade, and the situation could—if left alone—disintegrate into a bear market not unlike that of 1919–1920. Irving Fisher told a banking group that "any fears that the price level of stocks might go down to where it was in 1923 or earlier are not justified by present economic conditions." But what if they did? Who would rally the market then? Morgan was in his grave, and no one had replaced him. The Federal Reserve had been successfully challenged by Mitchell and others, and seemed ineffectual. President Hoover and Governor Roosevelt both disavowed the right to intervene. The market would be left to its own devices. Realizing this, the huge bull contingent switched to the bear side overnight. There were few optimists on Wall Street the next morning. Never before or since has such a rapid change in atmosphere taken place in the district.

Prices were lower Thursday morning, October 24, fell sharply, and never recovered. Volume for the first half-hour was 1,676,000 shares, a new record. By the end of the day, more than 12,895,000 shares were traded, also a record. That morning's *Times* had carried optimistic forecasts by business leaders. Mitchell was "still of the opinion that the reaction has badly overrun itself," and Lewis Pierson observed cryptically that "severe disturbances in the stock market are nothing new in American experience." These and other, similar statements, were being read as prices plummeted with no support in sight. A crowd rushed to the visitors' gallery overlooking the Exchange floor, where they witnessed bedlam. Some onlookers wept and others screamed—while the brokers themselves were in tears and hoarse with shouting. The gallery was closed at 11:00 to keep the hysterical from the scene and prevent riot. At the time more than $9 billion in paper values had been wiped out.

The Establishment could not stand by and allow such things to happen. Around noontime the city's leading bankers came in person or sent representatives to their headquarters: the offices of J. P. Morgan & Co. at 23 Wall Street. Thomas Lamont was there but Jack Morgan, still in Europe, was not. Albert Wiggin of Chase National, William Potter of the Guaranty Trust, Seward Prosser of Bankers Trust, and George F. Baker, Jr. of the First National appeared, as did Charles Mitchell. These men controlled more than $6 billion in assets, and were determined to stop the market decline. They would act for several reasons, not the least of which was their sense of responsibility. But there were other, more immediately practical considerations as well. Wiggin and Mitchell were both heavy speculators for their personal accounts; they and the others at the meeting were also entrapped in the brokers' loan market. If the decline were not halted, their institutions might be in danger.

In past panics, J. P. Morgan had taken charge, and his reputation and skill had stilled fears. None of these men had Morgan's reputation, but they did have money and intended to use it well. A pool of some $20–$30 million was raised to bolster the prices of key stocks. Richard Whitney, Exchange vice president and an ally of the House of Morgan, was named as their agent.

Whitney rushed from the meeting to the Exchange. Despite rumors that organized support was on the way, few noticed him at first. Whitney immediately went to the U. S. Steel post and asked its price. The last sale was at 205—*up* two points since the opening—but now the bid-ask price was a handful of points lower. In a loud, clear voice, Whitney bid 205 for 10,000 shares. Instantly those around him knew what had happened: Whitney represented a bull pool determined to stop the panic. They had chosen U. S. Steel as their vehicle. Steel was a key stock and also the proudest product of the House of Morgan. The bid had both real and symbolic meaning. As if to prove he would do still more, Whitney moved to other posts, shouting orders as he went. Cheers rose thunderously from the floor, and the word quickly spread to the streets. The market turned around and prices started to climb. Some stocks which had shown 10-point losses at noon ended the day with small gains. The panic—"Black Thursday"—seemed over and by 7:08 P.M., when the ticker finally stopped, it didn't appear too disastrous.

Selected Common Stocks, October 21–26, 1929

STOCK	OCT. 21	OCT. 22	OCT. 23	OCT. 24	OCT. 25	OCT. 26
American Can	159¾	161¼	154½	157½	155	153½
American Telephone	283	287	272	269	265¾	266
Eastman Kodak	223¾	233	218¼	219¾	226¾	223
General Electric	331	334	314	308	305½	297½
General Motors	59½	60¼	57⅜	53½	54	54¼
Goodrich	65	68	62½	60	60⅛	61⅞
International Harvester	105¼	109¾	100⅝	109½	103⅛	101¼
New York Air Brake	44⅝	45	42	40	41	41¼
Standard Oil (N.J.)	75⅞	77⅞	73½	68½	72	72¾
Union Pacific	258⅛	260	251⅜	252	55	256
United States Steel	210½	212⅛	204	206	204⅛	203¼

SOURCE: *New York Times,* October 22–27, 1929.

The *New York World* called it a "gamblers' panic," and other newspapers agreed. English economists John Maynard Keynes and Josiah Stamp argued that the decline might have been for the best, since it had liquidated unsound positions.

Keynes thought the money previously used for speculation would now be turned toward more productive enterprises. From Washington came President Hoover's comment that "the fundamental business of the country—that is, the production and distribution of goods and services—is on a sound and prosperous basis." Newspaper advertisements pointed out that not a single bank had fallen, not a single major concern was in trouble. Indeed, record earnings were reported by several large businesses, and it seemed certain that there would be a fine crop of year-end extra dividends. Stocks rose somewhat on Friday and declined on low volume Saturday morning.

The brief panic seemed over, and most observers hastily attempted to bury it and forget about Black Thursday. That Sunday's *Times* carried cheery statements from prominent businessmen in all parts of the nation, reporting that conditions were "sound." Eugene Stevens of the Continental Illinois Bank judged "There is nothing in the business situation to justify any nervousness," and even dour Alexander Dana Noyes observed that, unlike previous panics, there was no indication of business collapse. A major investment trust ran large ads in many newspapers, with a single word: "S-T-E-A-D-Y."

But the nation had not seen the end of the panic. Prices were lower Monday morning, destroying whatever optimism appeared on the surface. As stocks fell, the rumor market boomed. There were tales of another meeting at Morgan's; the suicides of several leading bankers; a huge bear pool organized by those former enemies, Cutten and Livermore; Mitchell going to Lamont to plead for a huge personal loan; Hoover paralyzed with fright. By 2:00 these rumors—all untrue—had their effect, as the selling continued and brokers attempted to dump their holdings.

A bankers' meeting did take place at 4:30, after trading had ended and while runners and clerks tried to straighten out their books. Thousands of margin calls were scheduled for the following morning, and hundreds of brokers began telephoning their clients to tell them the news. While Wall Street hummed with the noise of typewriters and the scurrying of runners, on Main Streets in all parts of the nation there was talk of margin calls, famous individuals who were trapped in vulnerable positions, and conspiracies to pull prices to a new low. "Caught short" became a standard answer to the cocktail party question, "How's things?"

Once again, the newspapers attempted to present the brighter side of the situation. The *Journal* thought Monday's session had seen a selling climax, after which prices would rise. "It was a panic, a purely stock-market panic, of a new brand," it said. But the investors—those who held stocks outright and not on margin —were still in fine shape. "They have lost a few tail feathers but in time they will grow again, longer and more luxurious than the old ones that were lost in what financial writers like to call the debacle." *The Times* believed "that the investor who purchases securities at this time with the discrimination that as always is a condition of prudent investing may do so with utmost confidence."

There was little confidence in evidence Tuesday morning. Volume for the first half hour was 3,260,000 shares, a record that would stand for more than thirty-five years. Prices fell all day, on a flood of sell orders, margin calls, and dumping. Late that night it was learned that 16,410,000 shares were exchanged on "Black Tuesday," a record which lasted for thirty-nine years. The Street heard of more bankers' meetings, possible intercession on the part of Washington, and a new bull pool being formed in the Midwest. None of these rumors made any difference, if indeed they were noted. The panic was on in earnest and reason dissolved into irrational impulses.

For the rest of their lives, brokers would tell stories about Black Tuesday to their juniors, in much the same fashion as old soldiers speak of battles in previous wars. Whenever a sharp decline took place in the future, there was bound to be an old-timer to tell of the days of '29. To be sure, the situation was grim; prices fell as never before. But these tales are only part of the truth. There were still no bank or major business failures; the suicide stories were grossly exaggerated (in fact, the suicide rate was *down* in this period) and corporate earnings were, indeed, hitting new highs as stocks struck their bottoms. If stocks were overvalued in July, they were undervalued in late October. Some realized this and began to buy (it is often forgotten that although more than 16.4 million shares were sold, the same number were bought) selectively. Floyd Odlum of Atlas Corporation made a fortune by bucking the market, as did Joseph Kennedy.

Selected Common Stocks, October 28–31, 1929

STOCK	OCT. 28	OCT. 29	OCT. 30	OCT. 31
American Can	136	120	131	135¾
American Telephone	232	204	240	246¾
Eastman Kodak	181¼	170	191¾	208¾
General Electric	250	222	247	252
General Motors	47½	40	49¾	48
Goodrich	60	55	55¾	56
International Harvester	87¾	80	93	95⅛
New York Air Brake	41	40	38	40¾
Standard Oil (N.J.)	64¾	57¾	65⅝	70¼
Union Pacific	240	239⅞	230½	242¾
United States Steel	186	174	185	193¼

SOURCE: *New York Times,* October 29–November 1, 1929.

As expected, there were the usual optimistic statements in the newspapers that night and the next morning. Hoover reiterated his belief that "the fundamental business of the country" was sound. U. S. Steel and American Can declared extra dividends. "The sun is shining again," wrote the *Journal*, "and we will go on record as saying some good stocks are cheap. We say good stocks are cheap because John D. Rockefeller said it first. Only the foolish will combat John D.'s judgement." To many it seemed that prices had fallen too rapidly; they might not rise to the pre-panic levels, but a correction did appear in order. Stocks rose sharply on Wednesday, October 30, and it seemed that indeed the worst was over. Brokers and customers, grasping at straws, viewed this first rally in a week as a sign of better things. After the close, Richard Whitney appeared to announce that the Exchange would open for a brief session Thursday and then remain shut until the following Monday, so as to clear up the huge backlog of business. There were cheers from the floor; Whitney's statement was taken as a sign that the Establishment was calling a halt to the panic.

The news was good during this intermission in trading. Assistant Secretary of Commerce Julius Klein told a radio audience that the economy was in fine condition. John D. Rockefeller issued a statement to the effect that he and his sons were buying stocks. Alfred Sloan of General Motors said "business is sound," and Henry Ford reduced the prices of his cars in a gesture of confidence. The Federal Reserve Bank of New York lowered the rediscount rate from 6 to 5 per cent, and many brokers announced they would carry margin customers even though they had deficits.

There was bad news as well. The Foshay complex of corporations, located in the Midwest, went bankrupt. Although the business was capitalized at more than $20 million, it had few connections with Wall Street banks, marketing its securities elsewhere. Foshay had counted on a new loan. Market conditions made this impossible, so the firm was forced to declare itself insolvent. Kreuger & Toll was obliged to cancel a bond issue, as were Bethlehem Steel and several other concerns. Warner Brothers and Paramount called off their merger, and similar stories dotted the business pages. Still, these firms were in good financial condition and the suspensions were thought temporary, to be reconsidered once matters were righted.

Brokers expected prices to rise on Monday, November 4, but instead they were hit by a flood of sell orders. The optimistic statements and forecasts of the previous days had obviously not worked to change the disillusionment with securities. The market was closed on Tuesday, Election Day, but then fell on Wednesday. "Trust God, not stocks," was the message of one prominent minister. Brokers advertised good bonds paying 7 per cent, but reported few takers. Money was drying up; the selling continued. Rockefeller attempted to support the price of Standard Oil of New Jersey by purchasing shares on the open market, with no success.

Selected Common Stocks, November 4–8, 1929

STOCK	NOV. 4	NOV. 5	NOV. 6	NOV. 7	NOV. 8
American Can	125	E	115	120	115¼
American Telephone	237	L	215	226	222
Eastman Kodak	193	E	173	183	181¾
General Electric	235	C	206	220	215
General Motors	45¼	T	40½	43½	43
Goodrich	55	I	55	52	52
International Harvester	90	O	80	81	80
New York Air Brake	40¾	N	39½	36¼	38⅛
Standard Oil (N.J.)	66½		61	63⅛	62
Union Pacific	235	D	215⅛	224½	221¾
		A			
		Y			

SOURCE: *New York Times,* November 5–9, 1929.

Prices fell on Wednesday, rose on Thursday, only to fall again on Friday. A pattern was developing of declines followed by weak rallies, followed once more by declines. By the third week in November, *The Times* and Dow-Jones Industrials were at their lowest points since July of 1927. By then the hectic activities of late October were over and Wall Street was shrouded in gloom, making attempts to understand what had happened. One investment bank said it better than most and was quoted in *The Times,* which paraphrased its market letter.

Certain theories of speculation have caught the public fancy in recent years and the liquidation of stocks has vividly illustrated the fallacies present in these theories, according to the semi-monthly financial review of Collins, Hall & Peckham. One of these, it is stated, was that no severe break was possible because of the presence of substantial investment trusts which, according to popular thought, would buy stock on any five per cent decline.

"Another belief that gained wide credence was that margin accounts were so well protected, in some cases as high as 50 to 60 per cent, that the trader on balance could never be wiped out," continues the review. "Three years ago a stock selling at ten times earnings was thought to have exhausted its possibilities; but three months ago the same stock, at twenty times earnings, was regarded as cheap. Business was considered so sound that sharp, protracted declines in stock quotations could not occur. . . .

"Just how far this technical recovery can carry is problematical, but we do not anticipate a sustained upswing in share prices. Market conditions should soon become normal, and we anticipate a greatly reduced volume of daily trading with far less violent price fluctuations."

10

Lost Opportunities

STOCK NEWS passed from the front pages by mid-November. Prices rallied from their lows, and ended the year in the midst of a subsided but strong market. The final figures for the year showed it to be above average in some respects.

Stocks of office equipment manufacturers, airlines, department stores, and steel companies generally did well in 1929, ending the year with advances. Auto companies, tobaccos, and meat packing declined. Ironically, amusement-related concerns were among the heaviest losers.

American Telephone & Telegraph scored a gain in 1929 (29½ points), as did American Can (12½ points), General Electric (22 points), and Standard Oil of New Jersey (11⅛ points). On the other hand, Goodrich fell 61½ points, and others, including International Harvester (16⅞ points), General Motors (40½ points), and Eastman Kodak (5½ points) were among the losers. High-flying R.C.A. dropped 43 points, and Nash Motors lost 55, to close at 54 on December 31. Chrysler's loss was 96 points, the stock falling to 36. The bare statistics, taken by themselves, seem to indicate a mixed-to-poor year for stocks, but not one that was disastrous.

On New Year's Day, 1930, *The Times* carried front-page stories of the deaths of seventy-two children in a fire in Scotland. Senator Smith Brookhart of Iowa called for the removal of Secretary of the Treasury Andrew Mellon—for failure to enforce Prohibition vigorously. Franklin Roosevelt was promised aid

Selected Common Stocks, November–December, 1929

STOCK	NOV. 9	NOV. 16	NOV. 23	NOV. 30	DEC. 7	DEC. 14	DEC. 21	DEC. 28
American Can	115¼	105½	116½	113	124¼	120	112¾	115¼
American Telephone	222	219⅞	223	223	233	222½	213	216⅜
Eastman Kodak	181¾	174¾	183½	175	196	181½	172½	174
General Electric	215	198	221	215½	250	239	226	229¼
General Motors	43	41¼	40⅜	39¼	41	43⅜	40¼	39⅞
Goodrich	52	48⅛	46¾	45¼	48½	48	43	40½
International Harvester	80	75¾	82	81	88½	82½	79½	76
New York Air Brake	38⅛	41	40¼	43	44	43¾	42	44½
Standard Oil (N.J.)	62	60¾	65	64	69¼	66⅜	62¾	64½
Union Pacific	221¾	218	225¼	225	227	221¾	216	212
United States Steel	171	164¼	167	162⅛	182¾	174	163	164½

SOURCE: *New York Times*, November 10–December 29, 1929.

Selected Common Stocks, 1929

VOLUME	STOCK	DIVIDEND	HIGH AND DATE		LOW AND DATE		CLOSE
13,463,300	American Can	$ 5.00	184½	Aug. 24	86	Nov. 13	122½
5,086,950	American Telephone	9.00	310½	Sept. 19	193¼	Jan. 8	222½
1,035,675	Eastman Kodak	8.00	264¾	Oct. 8	150	Nov. 13	177½
7,204,465	General Electric	6.00	403	Aug. 20	168⅛	Nov. 13	243½
29,837,200	General Motors	3.60	91¾	Mar. 21	33½	Oct. 29	40½
1,767,700	Goodrich	4.00	105¾	Jan. 2	38¼	Dec. 23	42
2,069,900	International Harvester	2.80	142	Aug. 30	65	Nov. 13	80½
269,700	New York Air Brake	3.60	49¾	Mar. 4	35½	Oct. 30	44⅛
14,329,700	Standard Oil (N.J.)	2.00	83	Sept. 16	48	Feb. 16	66⅛
698,900	Union Pacific	10.00	297⅝	Aug. 29	200	Nov. 13	216
20,336,700	United States Steel	8.00	261¾	Sept. 3	150	Nov. 13	171

SOURCE: *New York Times*, January 2, 1930.

by both Democrats and Republicans—for his New York pension program. There was no front-page story of the stock market, bank weaknesses, or business failures in that day's newspaper. One would have found it difficult to believe there had been a major crash two months earlier from a reading of the journals in early January.

Business leaders saw no reason for gloom that January 1. Frederick Ecker of Metropolitan Life admitted that the crash had been a bad experience, but predicted economic progress. "Any slackness that may be apparent in the general business situation during the early months of 1930 can be attributed almost entirely to the hesitant state of mind in which business has been since the collapse of the stock market, rather than to any important change in fundamental conditions." It was his opinion, and that of almost every other businessman interviewed, that the stock market crash was unrelated to business. The crash had punished the Outsiders and the foolish—people who believed in getting something for nothing. The producers of America were unharmed and would continue setting new records. Mellon agreed with this sentiment and was more outspoken than most in condemning the speculators, praising the sober businessmen and accepting the retribution and rewards which he believed would be meted out in the next year.

Let the slump liquidate itself. Liquidate labor, liquidate stocks, liquidate the farmers, liquidate real estate. . . . It will purge the rottenness out of the system. High costs of living and high living will come down. People will work harder, live a more moral life. Values will be adjusted, and enterprising people will pick up the wrecks from less competent people.

As for the pessimists of mid-1929, Roger Babson thought the crash had run its course, and that stock prices would rally in the new year. Alexander Noyes was less convinced of this. The crash had been "a reaction from an orgy of reckless speculation," he wrote. But the crash hadn't affected business: "No such excesses had been practiced by trade and industry. . . ." Noyes refused to predict the future. "We do not yet know whether this present episode is or is not an old-time 'major crisis.' "

Not even Noyes, the most farsighted of the market watchers of 1929, could imagine a new, major depression for the coming year. The worst that could happen, he thought, was a slump similar to that of 1919 or 1907.

To a generation raised believing that the 1929 panic led to the Great Depression, these words and the fairly calm economic atmosphere of early 1930 seem strange. The Antarctic explorations of Richard Byrd, and not the October crash, was singled out as the most important news story of 1929 by *The Times* editors early in 1930. The common stock of U. S. Steel was reorganized in 1929 and then fell more than 200 points in two months. Yet the company's president, James Farrell, declared an extra dividend and said: "It is confidently expected that after the turn of the year operations in the steel industry will substantially improve." Was this whistling in the dark—or were Farrell, and the many others like him, justified and honest in these thoughts?

A reading of the economic statistics of late 1929 and early 1930, along with the meanings drawn from them by businessmen and economists, would lead most to accept these and similar statements at face value. Economic and financial conditions in this period were no worse, and in some ways better, than those of other normal, slow years. The October crash on Wall Street had been unusual, even freakish. In the past, stock market panics had been precipitated by the failure of an important firm or bank. In the case of the 1901 panic, the decline was caused by a struggle for control of a railroad. But no major company failed in October 1929; the stories of huge bull and bear pools later proved exaggerated; no large industry seemed in economic difficulty; and there were no bank failures. Furthermore, previous panics had been stemmed by the arrival of a key individual, such as Alexander Hamilton in the 1792 panic and J. P. Morgan in 1907. By the early twenties, many sophisticated Wall Streeters thought the Federal Reserve, the investment trusts, the nature of the district's leadership, and the strength of the economy had made such people superfluous. While it was true that a consortium had been organized by the bankers in October, this group failed to prevent or reverse the crash. Instead, conditions righted themselves in mid-November—without the aid of anyone, so it seemed—vindicating those who had argued that the market was too strong to be crushed by a single person or event.

The market recovery and apparent economic stability of this period would give way not to new advances, but to a decade of depression. But no causal relationship between the events of late October 1929 and the Great Depression has ever been shown through the use of empirical evidence. Perhaps, then, the beliefs of those who held that panics *cum* depressions were a thing of the past were valid. If so, then the safeguards built into the financial structure after the death of Morgan in 1913 did work, and the eventual failure of the system should not be laid to the October crash, but to the lost opportunities of the next six months.

The key to any financial crash is the banking system. If banks can remain solvent and retain public confidence, then recovery may take place under their leadership. Every savior of the market in times of panic knew this, from Hamilton through U. S. Grant to J. P. Morgan. George Harrison, the new Governor of the New York Federal Reserve Bank, also recognized that his role would be vital in saving the financial structure in 1929–1930.

A shadowy individual during the early twenties, Harrison nonetheless was one of the more important figures in Federal Reserve circles. After a period as law clerk for Associate Justice Oliver Wendell Holmes, Jr., Harrison joined the legal staff of the Federal Reserve Board, where he caught Strong's eye early in 1920. Accepting an offer to become an officer in the New York Bank, the young Harrison was soon Strong's right-hand man. By 1928 he was Deputy Governor of the New

York Bank, handling much of the work for the ailing Strong. Thus, Harrison was no novice, though new to his post at the time the stock market began its wild gyrations in 1929.

Harrison faced a near impossible situation in the last two months of the year. Runs had begun on banks, and there was talk of panic followed by financial paralysis. It was thought that the banks and corporations which had made huge loans to brokers would now bring in these loans, resulting in thousands of margin calls, dumping of securities, lower prices, and then a repeat of the cycle. The Federal Reserve System could aid the banks through open market operations and manipulation of the rediscount rate, but the central bank was powerless to assist those individuals, corporations, and foreigners who had entered the brokers' loan market in force in 1928 and 1929. By early October these sources were more important than the banks, and more vulnerable. Harrison had managed to cut back on loans by banks early in 1929, but he and Governor Young had no control over the other sources. The market crash might easily cause many corporations to lose millions of dollars, become insolvent, and then draw upon banks and trust companies, which themselves would be dragged under. Naturally, the speculating public would also suffer through margin calls, and draw upon their reserves in the banks and trust companies. The Federal Reserve might save the financial structure from its own recklessness, but it could not do the same for nonmember banks and corporations, which had taken Professor Lawrence's and Charles Mitchell's advice to ignore the System.

Brokers' Loans by Source, 1928–1930 (*in millions*)

DATE	NEW YORK BANKS	OUTSIDE BANKS	OTHERS	TOTAL
June 30, 1928	$1,080	$960	$2,860	$4,900
Dec. 31, 1928	1,640	915	3,885	6,440
Oct. 4, 1929	1,095	760	6,640	8,525
Dec. 31, 1929	1,200	460	2,450	4,110

SOURCE: *Banking and Monetary Statistics, 1943.*

As the nonmember banks and corporations began to withdraw rapidly from the call money market, New York member banks entered to stabilize the situation. In October alone the New York banks took on an additional $1 billion in such loans, instructed their investment affiliates to hold back on margin calls, and in other ways attempted to halt the panic. Some of the money for this venture was acquired through rediscounting operations at the New York Federal Reserve Bank, and the rest by the sale of federal bonds. Thus, the member banks prevented a widespread panic in November, and were backed in this by the resources and leadership of the Federal Reserve.

But where did the central bank gain the authority for this operation? At the time, the Open Market Investment Committee was pledged to purchase not more than $25 million worth of short-term government notes a week. Such an amount would scarcely prevent a panic or aid banks in trouble. It was at this point that Harrison acted to fill the breach; he ordered the New York Bank to purchase an additional $160 million worth of short-term notes immediately, and continue this policy for as long as was necessary. By the end of November, Harrison had taken some $370 million of such securities, pumping a like amount of currency into the banks. Interest rates were maintained, as was liquidity; Harrison had saved the banking structure. When criticized by Young on the grounds that he lacked the authority for these actions, Harrison said, "It is not at all unlikely that had we not bought governments so freely, thus supplementing the reserves built up by large additional discounts, the stock exchange might have had to yield to the tremendous pressure brought to bear upon it to close on some one of those very bad days in the last part of October."

Harrison also acted to lower the rediscount rate, which went to 4½ per cent on November 14 and 4 per cent on January 20, 1930; by mid-March, the rate was 3½ per cent. This easy money policy, combined with open market operations, was instrumental in restoring a measure of confidence in November and December of 1929, and helped lead to the correction which lasted until the following April. It saved the banks. Contrary to popular belief today, the banks remained solvent during the crash; the wave of liquidations would not take place for another year.

Commercial Bank Suspensions, 1926–1932

YEAR	TOTAL FAILURES	MEMBER BANKS	NONMEMBER BANKS
1926	976	158	818
1927	669	122	547
1928	498	73	425
1929	659	81	578
1930	1,350	188	1,162
1931	2,293	516	1,777
1932	1,453	331	1,122

SOURCE: *Banking and Monetary Statistics, 1925–1933.*

Harrison's prompt and vigorous actions helped preserve the financial underpinnings of the American capitalist structure during the post-panic months. Had the expected recovery taken place, and had securities prices rallied as they did after 1926—a year when more banks failed than in 1929—Harrison would be remembered today as a hero of the period, the man who accomplished in 1929 what Morgan did in 1907 and 1893. But there was no recovery in mid-1930. The market broke downward in May and continued to slide for most of the rest of the year, as did key economic indicators. By January 1, 1931, there was no doubt that the nation was in a depression. Corporate

Key Economic Indicators, 1929–1932

YEAR	GROSS NATIONAL PRODUCT	WAGES	UNEMPLOYED	INVESTMENT AS A PERCENTAGE OF GNP
1929	$104.4 billion	$51.1 billion	1,550,000	15.2 per cent
1930	91.1 billion	46.8 billion	4,340,000	11.2 per cent
1931	76.3 billion	39.7 billion	8,020,000	7.1 per cent
1932	58.5 billion	31.1 billion	12,060,000	1.5 per cent

SOURCE: *1962 Supplement to Economic Indicators.*

profits, which reached $9.6 billion in 1929, fell to $3.3 billion in 1930. In 1931 American corporations lost $800 million, and a further decline to a $3 billion loss followed in 1932. Other figures were equally forbidding.

Common stocks also declined significantly.

Selected Common Stocks, 1930–1933

STOCK	JAN. 2, 1930	JAN. 2, 1931	JAN. 2, 1932	JAN. 2, 1933
American Can	119⅛	113¾	57¾	54⅞
American Telephone	220	181	112½	104⅛
Eastman Kodak	178⅛	151⅛	79	54¾
General Electric	242¼	45⅜	23¼	15¼
General Motors	40½	37⅜	20¾	13⅛
Goodrich	41	15¾	4	4½
International Harvester	79	50⅜	24	21⅛
New York Air Brake	44¼	21½	5	7
Standard Oil (N.J.)	65⅜	48⅞	27	30¼
Union Pacific	218	188	71	70⅝
United States Steel	167¼	142	37⅛	27½

SOURCE: *New York Times,* January 3, 1930–33.

Regular dividend payers like Anaconda, Bethlehem Steel, Westinghouse, Brooklyn Edison, and Northern Pacific suspended all payments, and most other stocks—American Telephone & Telegraph was a notable exception—reduced payouts. Still, in early 1933 one could receive a $6.00 dividend on Union Pacific, selling for around 70, and a $4.50 dividend on Air Reduction, which sold at 31. If it was true that stocks were too high in 1929, discounting not only the future but the hereafter as well, then prices were far too low in 1932, unless the investor assumed that the United States was doomed. Some did.

The reasons for this dismal picture may be found in the political paralysis of November 1929 to April 1930. Although there were weaknesses in the economy in this period, there was no depression. At the same time, the stock market seemed firm. Had those who possessed the power acted to shore up the economy, and those who controlled the Exchange and dominated American finance tried to correct abuses, the situation in mid-1930 might have been different. But Washington refused to act. President Hoover was as convinced as most that there would be no depression. On March 7, 1930, he told the nation that the economic picture was bright. There was some unemployment, he admitted, but this was confined to a few states and was temporary. Construction contracts showed an increase; new car sales were picking up. "All the evidence indicates that the worst effects of the crash upon unemployment will have been passed during the next sixty days." The Hoover Administration followed a hands-off policy while the economy began its taildive that spring.

The Exchange was equally inactive. Except for prohibiting nonbanking firms from entering the brokers' loan market, the Board of Governors did nothing. Speaking before a business group on January 25, President Simmons said:

It is obvious . . . that the high level of share prices last August rendered the stock market vulnerable to a considerable price decline. . . . Every serious break in the stock market is always attributed to over-speculation, but if we are to ascertain its exact responsibility for the 1929 stock panic we must consider the actual facts. . . . If mere volume of dealings or proportionate velocity of dealings on the Exchange were a cause of the panic, we should have had a panic not last fall but a year ago.

Thus, Simmons exonerated himself and the Exchange for its lack of strong action prior to the crash, and indicated that nothing in the way of reform could be expected in the future.

Richard Whitney spoke on the same subject on June 10. Better known than Simmons and more influential, Whitney represented the Establishment, the men who had lost power in the twenties, then went along with the chicanery of the Outsiders, and finally failed to halt the decline. Like Simmons, Whitney was convinced that he and his group had nothing more to do.

No one, I am sure, likes panics. No one certainly likes periods of excessive liquidation in the securities markets, least of all those of us whose lives and fortunes have been devoted to the security business. But if we must face such periods of adversity, we must do so boldly and like men. And the events of last autumn have increased in us not only this realization, but also our faith in this marvelous country of ours, and our confidence that in its financial market places even the utmost periods of stress and the days of most bitter adversity cannot long check or withstand our inevitable onward economic progress.

In testimony before the Senate Committee on Banking and Currency, Charles Mitchell and Albert Wiggin would admit to having speculated in their banks' securities; both men subsequently faced prosecution. Richard Whitney would be found guilty in criminal court of having misused company funds in 1937—and sent to prison. The period which began with a poor, naïve, and plausible Italian ex-smuggler, Charles Ponzi, being incarcerated for attempting to bilk the public, ended with Richard Whitney, the scion of one of America's most distinguished families, and a member of the Wall Street Establishment, in jail for similar reasons.

Conclusion

DURING THE twenties the stock market became the focus of much popular interest. Along with Prohibition and baseball, it was the subject of conversation at private meetings throughout the nation. To many it seemed a perfect reflection of the new industrial America which had emerged from the Great War the most powerful nation in the world. Others considered it symbolic of the dangerous frivolity of the period, a hedonistic institution which would lead the country to ultimate destruction. Neither was true. Instead, the great bull market, the increased public interest, and the use of credit and leverage, appeared to fit the people's demands for a larger share in the progress made during the decade. That there were abuses and distortions cannot be denied, but neither can one conclude that the bull market should not have taken place, or that investor enthusiasm was unjustified.

It has been said that the most sorrowful word in the English language is "if." In retrospect, the word comes to mind quite often. If the Federal Reserve System had been less timid in the early part of the decade, many abuses in the call money market might have been avoided. If Andrew Mellon had been less concerned with correcting what he considered evil laws and policies of the Progressive era, and had a better knowledge of economics and less of a dedication to the business community's short-range goals, he might have proposed different types of tax reforms. If labor and the farmer had received higher wages and returns for their products, then the economy would have been stronger, and better able to cope with recessions. If businessmen had not become convinced that credit was the only key to prosperity, and the consumer was made to see that credit [time purchases] could destroy as well as create, it might not have been abused. If Charles Mitchell had not declared his independence of the Federal Reserve or had been checked by Benjamin Strong or Roy Young, then the great rise and fall of 1928–1929 might have been avoided. If Strong had not placed so high a priority on aiding the pound sterling, then raises in the rediscount rate might have curbed the public's appetite for margin purchases. If the bankers' consortium had been stronger and more persistent, then the panic might have been stopped in late October. If George Harrison's brave and intelligent use of Federal Reserve resources had been followed by effective action from the Exchange Board of Governors and Washington, then the panic might not have been followed by the depression.

The list of lost opportunities and mistakes of the period could be extended almost indefinitely. It should be remembered, however, that all of this can be seen only in retrospect. The leading figures of the period may have been foolish and short-sighted, but for the most part they were not evil or stupid. Charles Mitchell was self-serving but, as he later observed, he caused the destruction of no man directly—although indirectly he was in part responsible for the crash. Andrew Mellon was called the greatest Secretary of the Treasury since Hamilton—until 1930. Benjamin Strong remains one of the great central bankers in American history—although his reputation might have suffered had he not died in 1928. Calvin Coolidge was guilty of many errors of omission, but a too-often maligned Herbert Hoover receives much of the blame for the events of 1929–1932. Men like Alexander Dana Noyes, the clearest student of the market in the twenties, are almost forgotten. Few remember George Harrison, whose brief moment in the sun showed him to be a banker of intelligence and fortitude.

Conditions might have been strikingly different had Hoover

been elected president in 1924 instead of 1928, and had Harrison been in charge of the New York Federal Reserve Bank a few years earlier than 1928. These ruminations do not belong to the realm of history, but they are discussed by students of the period. It is only human to think such thoughts, wondering why problems developed and how they might have been avoided.

As Wall Street came to recognize its problems and short-comings, attempts were made at reform. Brokers were obliged to accept a code of conduct which was promulgated in May 1930. Later in the year, the Exchange spearheaded a drive to rid the district of incompetent and shady customers' men. Several securities were delisted for irregularities, among them Brockway Motors and Allied Chemical & Dye. In general, however, the Exchange and the Wall Street community did little to clean house. In early 1932, the district seemed moribund and discredited. Cutten, Raskob, the Fisher brothers, and other great figures of the twenties were almost forgotten. Professor Lawrence was gone, and Irving Fisher's attempts to explain his errors were generally ignored. Their places were taken by a new group of speculators and analysts. Just as the late twenties had seen the greatest bull speculators in American history, so the early thirties was the great age of Wall Street bears.

The leading bear was Bernard E. Smith, better known as "Sell 'Em Ben." Smith was in his early forties in 1930. He had gone from the Hell's Kitchen section of New York to a broker's office, and then left Wall Street to serve as a sailor. Smith sold cars and did other odd jobs during World War I. He returned to Wall Street in the early twenties and became office manager for an Exchange firm. During the next nine years he participated in pools, hob-nobbed with the great bulls, and learned the ropes. Then, in 1929, he began to think of organizing bear pools. Legend has it that Smith ran into his broker's office on Black Tuesday screaming, "Sell 'em all! They're not worth anything!" and so gained his nickname. By 1931 Smith was making $10 million a month for his group on short sales, and was the most feared bear on the Street.

Smith became the symbol of the bears, but in reality he was only one of many. His partner, Tom Bragg, made fortunes by selling American Telephone & Telegraph short at the right time. Percy Rockefeller was one of the shrewdest bears of the day. William Danforth became a millionaire through his bear manipulations. Joseph Kennedy made much of his fortune in this period through short sales. Even these men, however, shared the general terror of what the future would bring, as prices fell with no end in sight. "I am not ashamed to record that in those days I felt and said I would be willing to part with half of what I had if I could be sure of keeping, under law and order, the other half," was Joseph Kennedy's later comment on his fears of those days in the early thirties.

From their beginnings, the securities markets had been self-regulating. To be sure, Washington and Albany had placed restrictions on some aspects of the market but, for the most part, these were ignored, manipulated, or actually written by district leaders themselves. The 1929 crash changed all this. Unable to cope with the depression, finance capitalism conceded that it lacked powers formerly ascribed to the private sector of the economy. Leadership would have to come from another quarter. "We may as well tell the truth and put the blame where it belongs," sighed William C. Durant. "It's up to Washington now. We have stepped aside. The market is leaderless." Durant thought the problems transitory. "Eventually we will take control again. . . ." he said, but Durant would not guess as to when this would happen.

Many early New Dealers considered the problems being discussed on Wall Street and came up with their own answers and conclusions. It appeared to them that the great crash had been caused by excesses on the part of Wall Street, and the depression had been brought on by the crash. Accordingly, they seemed to believe that prosperity might return when these abuses were corrected. This was a key element of New Deal thinking in 1933.

The Securities Act of 1933 gave the Federal Trade Commission powers to oblige investment bankers to follow prescribed methods in offering and advertising securities. The Glass-Steagall Act established the Federal Deposit Insurance Corporation to safeguard depositors, and ordered commercial banks to divest themselves of their investment affiliates. Finally, the Securities and Exchange Commission was established to "put a policeman at the corner of Wall Street and Broad," to prevent those actions which had led to the crash. Other legislation followed, all designed to curb Wall Street.

Spokesmen for the financial community protested some of these acts—especially the SEC—while accepting other New Deal legislation as fair and necessary. More important, they denied culpability in causing the depression. Although Wall Street presented a good case in the years that followed, few took it seriously. The financial district had been the symbol of prosperity in the 1920s, a prosperity which could have existed without the bull market. There is no record of any major Wall Street leader rejecting this role. To the generation of the Great Depression, it appeared that Wall Street had caused many, if not all, the problems facing the nation. Few bankers were willing to accept as much blame as they deserved.

Both judgments were exaggerated and, to a large degree, false. The markets of the 1920s were mirrors for prosperity, just as those of the 1930s were reflections of depression.

Bibliographical Essay

BEFORE BEGINNING a study of the securities markets, one should try to capture the flavor of the period. Only then can the reader understand the men and forces which made the bull market possible. A good start would be Preston Slossen's *The Great Crusade and After* (New York, 1937), which dramatizes the falling away from Wilsonian idealism in the decade. Frederick Lewis Allen's *Only Yesterday* (New York, 1961) is the most famous work by an evocative historian of the period. *Masks in a Pageant* (New York, 1928) by William Allen White deserves mention because of its author's prominent position and his closeness to political leaders of the twenties. The same could be said of the last two volumes of Mark Sullivan's masterpiece, *Our Times,* five volumes (New York, 1927). David Shannon's short but insightful *Between the Wars: America, 1919–1941* (New York, 1965) is also recommended as is William Leuchtenburg's *The Perils of Prosperity* (New York, 1958).

George Soule's *Prosperity Decade* (New York, 1947) remains the best economic history of the period. Financial problems are surveyed in Paul Studenski and Herman Krooss, *Financial History of the United States* (New York, 1963). *Benjamin Strong: Central Banker* (Washington, 1958) is Lester Chandler's sympathetic treatment of the man whom the author considers one of America's major financial figures. Relevant sections of Milton Freedman and Anna Schwartz, *A Monetary History of the United States, 1867–1960* (Princeton, 1963) are more critical of Strong, and this book is one of the few that discusses Federal Reserve actions during 1929–1930 in detail, especially the role played by George Harrison. Seymour Harris, *Twenty Years of Federal Reserve Policy,* two volumes (Cambridge, 1933), is not as enlightening for a student of the securities markets. Elmus R. Wicker, *Federal Reserve*

Monetary Policy, 1917–1933 (New York, 1966), is a pioneering work which will appeal to the advanced student of the subject.

Any study of the stock market in the twenties should include Alexander Dana Noyes' *The War Period of American Finance, 1908–1925* (New York, 1926). The reader would do well to go into Noyes' earlier work, *Forty Years of American Finance, 1865–1907* (New York, 1909). Historians will learn much from these volumes, although the author's terminology may be difficult at times. *The Big Board* by Robert Sobel (New York, 1965) is a history of the New York stock market from its beginning to the present. Dana Thomas' *The Plungers and the Peacocks* (New York, 1967) is the most recent history of the market.

Individuals and events of the market in the twenties can best be studied through newspapers and magazines. The most important of these are the *Saturday Evening Post, Collier's, Life, Business Week, Commercial and Financial Chronical, Banker's Magazine,* and the *Literary Digest,* all of which printed articles on the stock market from time to time. The financial pages of *The New York Times,* the *Wall Street Journal,* and the New York *Sun* were invaluable in my researches, and no student should neglect *Forbes* or *Barron's.*

There are many excellent books on the subject as well. Forrest McDonald's *Insull* (Chicago, 1962) is a major work, which is sympathetic toward its subject and offers clear and insightful chapters on the Insull empire. Allen Churchill's *The Incredible Ivar Kreuger* (New York, 1957) is racy and revealing; Harvey O'Connor's *Mellon's Millions* (New York, 1933) is a muckraking job, and Earl Sparling's *Mystery Men of Wall Street* (New York, 1930) is generally accurate although presented in a flamboyant manner. Also of interest is *High and Low Financiers* (Indianapolis, 1932) by Watson Washburn and Edmund De Long, which contains chapters on some minor figures of the period. Interesting material can be found in Arthur Wickwire, *The Weeds of Wall Street* (New York, 1933); Richard Wycoff, *Wall Street Ventures and Adventures through Forty Years* (New York, 1930); A. Newton Plummer, *The Great American Swindle, Inc.* (New York, 1932); Ferdinand Lundberg, *America's 60 Families* (New York, 1937); and Edward Dies, *Behind the Wall Street Curtain* (Washington, 1952).

Bull market psychology before the 1929 crash can be fathomed by reading Joseph Stagg Lawrence, *Wall Street and Washington* (Princeton, 1929) and Charles Dice, *New Levels in the Stock Market* (New York, 1929). Joe Alex Morris, *What a Year!* (New

York, 1956) is a lively though superficial treatment of the events of 1929.

There are several worthwhile books on the crash. The best of these is Noyes' *The Market Place* (Boston, 1938), a memoir which contains a study of the panic, an analysis of its causes, and vignettes of the period. Frederick Lewis Allen's *The Lords of Creation* (New York, 1935), is somewhat better than *Only Yesterday* on this subject, and contains some of the author's finest writing. John Kenneth Galbraith's *The Great Crash* (Boston, 1955) is the most famous book on the panic, but not the best. Galbraith has drawn heavily upon Allen and Noyes for his material and has written the book partly to prove that it could happen again, a case he does not substantiate convincingly. Still, the wit and style of this book, as well as the author's reputation, make it required reading. Lionel Robbins' *The Great Depression* (New York, 1934) is more interesting from the economist's point of view, as is Maurice Lee's *Economic Fluctuations: Growth and Stability* (Homewood, Illinois, 1959), and United States, 74th Congress, 1st Session, Senate Committee on Banking and Currency, *Stock Exchange Practices* (Washington, 1933). Giulio Pontecorvo, "Investment Banking and Security Speculation in the Late 1920's," *Business History Review*, XXXII (Summer, 1958), 166–91, is an excellent short study of selected aspects of the stock market in the period, which cannot be ignored by any serious student of the subject. Hugh Bullock's *The Story of Investment Companies* (New York, 1959), which clearly explains the leverage structures in investment trusts, completes this bibliography.

It remains to be said that several books should be on this list, but unfortunately have not yet been written. There is no study of the Van Sweringens, or of Charles Ponzi. George Harrison has been ignored by biographers; I could find little about him in most works on the Federal Reserve System. There are no biographies of Charles Mitchell, Thomas Lamont, and other bankers of the era. No one has investigated corporate financing and securities reorganizations in a full-length study. Winston Churchill's career as Chancellor of the Exchequer has been the subject of some monographs, but it deserves a more complete book, as does the economic philosophy of Andrew Mellon. James Prothro's *The Dollar Decade* (New York, 1954) is a fine study of business ideology in the twenties, but more is needed along these lines.

Appendix

Growth in Twenty-Five Largest Firms, 1917–1929
(figures in millions of dollars)

RANK 1917	RANK 1929	COMPANY	ASSETS 1917	ASSETS 1929	REVENUES 1917	REVENUES 1929	NET INCOME 1917	NET INCOME 1929
1	1	U. S. Steel	2,450	2,296	1,285	1,097	224.2	197.5
2	2	Standard Oil (N.J.)	574	1,767	412	1,523	80.8	120.9
30	3	General Motors	134	1,131	173	1,504	27.7	247.3
36	4	Standard Oil (Ind.)	127	847	190	495	25.4	83.0
3	5	Bethlehem Steel	382	802	299	343	27.3	42.2
20	6	Ford Motor	160	761	275	1,143	30.3	88.4
14	7	Standard Oil (N.Y.)	204	708	N.A.	N.A.	21.8	38.8
13	8	Anaconda Copper	216	681	156	306	34.3	69.1
33	9	Texas Corp.	129	610	54	213	19.7	48.3
35	10	Standard Oil (Calif.)	127	605	79	190	19.0	46.6
10	11	General Electric	232	516	197	415	26.9	67.3
7	12	E. I. du Pont	263	497	270	200E	45.6	72.3
—	13	Shell Union Oil*	—	486	—	245	—	17.6
4	14	Armour & Co.	314	452	577	1,000	21.3	9.8
49	15	Gulf Oil	103	431	71	272	16.7	44.5
69	16	Sinclair Oil	81	401	45	197	9.1	16.6
6	17	International Harvester	265	384	166	337	14.0	36.6
5	18	Swift & Co.	306	351	875	1,000E	34.6	13.1
25	19	Kennecott Copper	143	338	23	116	18.0	52.1
43	20	Republic Steel	112	332	78	N.A.	15.9	20.5
26	21	Pullman	141	316	49	N.A.	13.6	17.7
54	22	Western Electric	96	309	152	411	2.9	27.0
9	23	U. S. Rubber	250	308	176	193	15.3	0.6
21	24	Union Carbide & Carbon	157	307	N.A.	142	9.6	33.7
71	25	International Paper	80	283	N.A.	N.A.	8.9	2.7

* Organized in 1922.
SOURCE: *Forbes,* Vol. 100, No. 6 (Sept. 15, 1967), pp. 54–57.

Index

WATERLOO HIGH SCHOOL LIBRARY
1464 INDUSTRY RD.
ATWATER, OHIO 44201

The great Bull Market   12039
Sobel, Robert   332.6 Sob